GASPORT
girl

d. jean lang

Order this book online at www.trafford.com
or email orders@trafford.com

Most Trafford titles are also available at major online book retailers.

Print information available on the last page.

ISBN: 978-1-5539-5578-8 (sc)

Trafford rev. 04/10/2023

www.trafford.com
North America & international
toll-free: 844-688-6899 (USA & Canada)
fax: 812 355 4082

DEDICATION

To my loving grandmother, Mary Ann Degan, a positive role model who gave me unconditional love.

THE DEGANS

WARM FEELINGS

Sinking down into the feather mattress of the big black four-poster bed, I could hear the voices downstairs of my grandmother and uncle. The smell of bacon frying and coffee boiling made me feel warm and secure. All was well this summer morning of 1940 in Gasport, New York. The voices rose and fell as I heard the clatter of pots and pans in the big kitchen at the rear of the house. This house that my grandfather had built mostly by himself, as I was told.

I eased out from under the covers into the chilly morning air of the bedroom put on my socks, shoes, sweatshirt and pants and hurried down the steps to the warm kitchen. The toilet facilities consisted of an outhouse some distance from the rear of the house. My grandfather had built that also. It was in the style of the house with a slanted roof and painted the same color. Today it would resemble a children's playhouse. He had constructed a cement sidewalk from the rear of the house at the bottom of the steps out to the outhouse. The sidewalk also encircled the house from the wide covered front porch to the rear porch/shed just outside the kitchen door. I didn't really mind this trip in the summer but visiting during Christmas or other colder holidays, it took quite a bit of courage to get dressed and brave the weather just to go to the bathroom. We had pitchers of water and bowls in the bedrooms for washing, and to take baths my grandmother would heat a giant copper kettle on the large kitchen wood-fired cook stove.

Entering the warm kitchen I was greeted by my grandmother with a big smile. My Uncle Emmett was sitting on top of the far end of the cook stove also smiling and joking with my grandmother. Emmett was the baby of the family and he enjoyed the reputation of a teaser and party goer.
"Come over here, Jeanie. Tell me if you think I need to shave." At that he picked me up and rubbed his scratchy beard up against my smooth cheek.
"Ouch, gramma…?." I pleaded…as he threw his head back in gales of laughter.

"Emmett, leave her alone now," Gramma said without rancor.
The kitchen was rectangular shaped with the large black iron cook stove between the two back windows that looked out onto the sloping yard in the rear. On the end furthest from the door was another window looking out onto the side driveway and a full-flowered lilac bush. Next to this was a kitchen table in one corner with three chairs next to it and Gramma's rocking chair in front of the window. To the right of the entrance of the kitchen was a sink with a counter top and a metal pump that brought water from the cistern in the basement. We didn't drink this water, it was only for washing ourselves or dishes.

Grampa had come into the kitchen and quietly put a mirror on the upper windowsill and turned down the collar of his shirt to prepare to shave. There was a teakettle full of hot water on the stove which he used to fill the white metal basin in the sink. He did not speak. All 5 feet 5 inches of him stood in front of the mirror where his completely bald head reflected the light bulb hanging from the ceiling. Most of the time he covered it with a brown well-worn bowler hat. His pants were held up with suspenders and were tucked into knee-high rubber boots. The long sleeves of his cotton shirt were rolled up to his elbows. This was his constant attire for as long as I can remember him.

"What would you like for breakfast, Jeanie?" Gramma said. I knew that it would be a large cup of freshly brewed coffee with canned milk and sugar and toast. Gramma made toast on the griddle of the cook stove and I loved the burnt taste as big wedges of butter melted into it. Soon there would be fresh strawberries from the neighbor's garden.

Emmett had on a white sweatshirt and khaki pants. His reddish blond hair was seldom combed but looked as though he just pushed it back with his fingers. He slid down off the stove and announced, "Okay, guess I'll go out and cause some trouble." as he looked smiling at Gramma.

"Be gone with you before I spank you right here in front of Jean." At that he swung around and picked all 4 feet 11 inches of her off her feet and swung her around as her pure white hair that was pulled back into a bun started to unravel down her neck. She loved it. He grabbed me again and rubbed his beard across my cheek again.

"EMMETT....GRAMMA...make him stop." Grampa never blinked an eye but just kept shaving the white lather off his face with his straight razor. He sharpened the razor on a long black razor strop he had hung from the sink. Gramma had Emmett very late in her life. She was now 73 and Emmett was only in his twenties. Of course I didn't even think about it then. I just knew he was great fun and loved it when he threw me up in the air and caught me coming down. I had been the only grandchild to spend time here with my grandparents so far. After being the only child of my parents for almost seven years, my sister Joanne was born followed thirteen months later by another sister, Mary Ann. I delighted in still being "the favorite" here in this house where I did not have to share the spotlight with anyone else.

Since I was very young (I was told), I was brought down to Gasport to spend the summers and vacations with Gramma, Grampa and the two uncles still living at home. At home in Buffalo I lived a totally different life. We lived in South Buffalo in a very diverse neighborhood with first generation, Italians, Poles and Germans. I rode city buses, went to public school and even at 8 years old was doing grocery shopping for my mother at the local shops. Friends my age lived in almost every house near me, and I never lacked for friends to play with or go to the movies with.

Here in Gasport, there were mostly adults. And while I was loved as a child, I felt treated like another adult. My opinions were listened to and Gramma talked with me as if I were her best friend. I think I might have been.

"Come here to the table and eat your breakfast" Gramma said.

Thinking back I can't believe I downed those giant cups of strong coffee. I probably only weighed 60 pounds and must have been wired all day. There was usually more coffee with lunch and dinner. It's a wonder I ever slept.

Grampa had finished shaving and Emmett had left the house. Just Gramma and I were alone in the kitchen.

"Did you have any dreams?" Gramma inquired. This was a ritual of almost every morning. The Irish are fervent believers in dreams and "things that go bump in the night." Actually, I always seemed to have a dream to relate. Must have been all that coffee. Gramma would then interpret the dream. Then she would begin with stories from the past.

"You know we lived in a house in Hulberton and at night we would hear noises and when we got up in the morning the furniture would be moved in different places. Sometimes the fire would be put out in the fireplace even though we left a good stock of wood burning,"

Shivers would go up and down my spine. I pictured wispy ghosts flying through the house at night moving furniture and putting out fires. I would ask to sleep with Gramma tonight instead of in my own big bed in the other room. Once in awhile she would give in.

IRISH ROOTS

Grampa Thomas Degan was born in Manchester, England 74 years ago. His Irish parents Patrick and Elizabeth Whalen Degan were born in 1845 and 1847 respectively. Like many Irish families, they went across the Irish Sea to England for work. They emigrated to America during the Potato Famine. They came to America and settled in Western New York where many including my grandfather went to work on building the Erie Barge Canal (as it was known in those days). I was told that Grampa's mother, Elizabeth, opened a hotel in Orangeport on the Canal. I do know that somewhere Grampa learned to be a mason (bricklayer), carpenter, electrician and built this family home in Gasport. He did all the carpentry, masonry and electrical work. Before unions came into being. He also brought with him from Ireland the seedling for the now large horse chestnut tree which stands over 50 feet tall in the front of the house. The other trees around the house, two sweet cherry and three sour cherry trees, he also planted. It seemed to me that there was nothing he could not do. With the exception of making peace with Gramma.

Grampa Degan was now 74 years old and had made himself a room in the basement. He still slept in the front bedroom of the house, shaved every morning in the kitchen, and sat in the big overstuffed chair in the living room smoking his pipe during the day. But he and Gramma rarely spoke to each other. Gramma slept in one of the five upstairs' bedrooms. Uncle Eddie still a bachelor had his own bedroom in the front of the upstairs and Uncle Emmett was also still living at home.

Gramma and Grampa had 13 children, 12 biological (7 boys, 5 girls) and one female cousin raised by them. The fact that my grandparents did not talk to each other was a constant mystery to me. Here and there, since I was usually surrounded by adults, I gleaned that there had been a falling out some years previously. The story went that my Uncle Eddie was rather indulged by Gramma. He drove a truck for the local lumberyard and after work spent much time at the local tavern, The Hammond Hotel. Gramma would keep his meals waiting for him to come home no matter how late he arrived. Apparently, there was a standoff between Gramma and Grampa about this and Grampa said he would no longer eat at the table while Gramma waited for Eddie.

Now one needs to know that Grampa Degan was among other things the epitome of stubbornness. One scenario I overhead concerned the time when the post office began delivering mail to the houses on our street. Prior to that it was necessary to walk almost a mile up to the post office to get one's mail. Grampa built a beautiful wooden mailbox and erected it in front of the house, but the post office said it would not deliver mail to it because it was not "regulation size." He needed to purchase a regulation sized mail box. Not Grampa. He took the whole thing down and we were the only family on East Avenue without a mailbox. Instead he rented a box at the local post office.

Actually, this trek to the post office, sometimes twice a day, took up quite a lot of my vacation time in Gasport. I also had to pick up the two newspapers at the drugstore every day. My Grandmother was an avid reader of both the Lockport Union Sun & Journal and the Buffalo Evening News. Both papers were delivered by Greyhound Bus every day to Joneses' drugstore in Gasport. For my afternoon trip up to the drugstore, Gramma gave me 35 cents, 25 cents for a chocolate marshmallow sundae and 10 cents for a Coca Cola. Mr. and Mrs. Jones, owners and operators of the drugstore, were my idols. Mrs. Grace Jones was an attractive woman in her 40's or 50's with short gray curly hair. She was always impeccably dressed with a broad smile showing perfectly white teeth. Mr. Jones was the pharmacist and also sundae maker. He always wore a sparkling clean white coat and his dark hair was slicked down in a conventional way.

"What's it today, Jean, the usual?" he smiled.

Thomas Degan & Eugene McCollum -Front Porch)

(Mirror Lake -Gasport)

Sunday in Gasport on Front Porch - Friends and Family - 1938

(Top Row: Left to right: Jacob Yerge, Sr., Grace (Degan) Yerge, Tom Brady, Mary Ann Degan, Harold Roche, Peter Gormley)

(Bottom Row: Mary Gormley, Baby Nancy Gormley, Bill Degan, Margaret Gormley, D. Jean Kolb in front)

"Chocolate marshmallow sundae and a coke," I replied.

He smiled as he expertly scooped the vanilla ice cream from the cardboard tub behind the counter. After the chocolate syrup and white marshmallow were dripping down the sides of the ice cream, he would add a bright red cherry in the middle.

"There you go. Enjoy".

And did I ever. I can still taste those sundaes and the sweet bubbly Coca Cola. By the time I was finished, the Greyhound bus would come pulling up in front of the store with squealing brakes. Other people were also waiting for the newspapers to read about the latest world events. Germany had invaded Poland in 1939, Britain had declared war on Germany and all of Europe and America were expecting the worst as Hitler continued his quest for power. The newspapers were handed out to all the folks waiting, including me, and I was off down the street back home enjoying the memory of my sundae without concern for the world situation. Instant television news in our living rooms was ten years away for most of us.

I cut through the side yard of The Hammond Hotel, crossed the railroad tracks next to the train station, passed Standish Lumber Yard where Uncle Eddie worked, and headed down East Avenue. There was a sidewalk on one side of the street across from Friend's Manufacturing Company. Started by the mostly Quaker inhabitants of Gasport, it seemed to be a thriving business. Further down the street, I passed St. Mary's Catholic Church where we went on Sundays to Mass. In the winter if there was no coal for the furnace, a sign would be hung on the front of the church door, "NO COAL. NO MASS." So we would have to walk the three-quarters of a mile back home in the frozen wind. The priest, Father Donnelley, who looked strangely like the movie priest, Barry Fitzgerald, was an irascible soul who scolded us every Sunday, and ridiculed the poorly painted and decorated church. We were all too afraid to question him and simply sat and felt bad. Gasport only had a hundred or so Catholic families in the town and the priest only came for one Sunday mass every week from the neighboring larger community of Middleport's St. Stephen's Church. According to stories from my family, my uncles and aunts suffered and fought much prejudice at school because of being Irish Catholic.

Further down the street, the sidewalk ended, and then I had to walk on the side of the road. At the top of the hill there were no trees to block the bright summer sun, and I hurried along to reach the foot of the hill and shelter of the horse chestnut trees.

MARY ANN (CONNERS) DEGAN

My grandmother was my idol. At less than 5 feet tall, she could do almost anything. Born in 1867 in Gasport of Irish parents who had emigrated from County Cork, Ireland she had met and married my grandfather. The thirteen children they had were mostly raised by Gramma while Grampa spent long hours working on the canal and the railroad. Working on the railroad entailed being away in different cities for weeks at a time. Sometimes he wouldn't be back home for six months. So Gramma had to become self-sufficient.

Everyday I watched as she would lift a heavy steel bucket of fresh water from the outside well and hoist it up on the side of the kitchen sink. I couldn't even lift it, much less get it up onto the sink. She chopped wood for the kitchen cook stove, and each morning got up and started a fire in the stove with the kindling wood she gathered the night before.

By 1940 she had buried four of my uncles. The oldest, my Uncle William, had served in World War I and suffered from gas inhalation and died after returning home. Uncle Harold, not a well child from the beginning, had succumbed to respiratory problems. Uncle Leslie ("Let") had died in the hospital of pneumonia--before the use of antibiotics such as penicillin. The youngest and most tragic death was my Uncle Johnny. He had been a passenger in the rumble seat of a car full of young boys that went out of control and landed in the Erie Canal. His neck was broken and he never recovered. Gramma rarely spoke of these incidents, yet she must have suffered greatly with all these losses.

With me she was tender and loving and listened to my questions and concerns for hours on end. *Unconditional positive regard* I learned later in life is what it is called. I would sit on her lap for what seemed like hours as she would gently push the old rocking chair back and forth. Her white hair was usually pulled back into a bun on the back of her head, but on occasion she would let me take it down and comb it. This was one of my great delights, and it never occurred to me how this might not have been equally enjoyable to her.

She never scolded me although I'm sure I must have done something wrong. My goal was to please her and continue to be loved. I didn't want to do anything to offend or displease her. The few times she "corrected" me I never forgot.

It was a hot summer. "Gramma, I am SO HOT."

"Jean, a lady is never "hot", you are "warm." she gently reminded me.

I couldn't for the life of me then understand the difference except to think that warm was surely not as hot as "hot". But I never used the term "hot" again to refer to how I was feeling.

She always wore a clean starched colorful apron upon which would be hanging a string of safety pins. Her dresses reached to her ankles and the top of her sturdy black shoes. Sturdy enough to step on a snake if we saw one in the grass and crush its head. Meanwhile I was cringing behind her as I heard the crunching noise. When she would serve me lunch or dinner at the big oak dining room table, I sat at the head of the table. I used to ask her which place each of my aunts and uncles used to sit at during mealtime. This must have also been painful for her to recall, but she pointed out the place of each one. And I had visions of all the laughter and conversation that must have gone on between these thirteen siblings. In some ways I wished I had been one of them, but in another I was glad now to be the only one here.

Another "correction" occurred around mealtime. As I began to comment on one of the vegetables I was served, I heard my grandmother's voice.

"Jean, you must always *respect* your food," she spoke quietly.

Although I wasn't sure exactly what that meant, I knew what she had taught me about respecting my elders. But that type of respect came with words, 'thank you very much', 'pleased to meet you', 'sorry', 'excuse me.' What could I *say* to this food to show respect. How does one *respect* a carrot?

THE VISIT

After breakfast dishes were cleared and put away, it was time to "go visiting". She would take off her apron, brush any strands of hair that fallen astray and we would head out the side kitchen door. Before we left, she would coach me on what to say and how to behave.

Our next door neighbor, who only lived just the other side of our outside pump and his driveway, was Mr. Dickinson. I never learned his first name because she called him "Mr. Dickinson" and he called her, "Mrs. Degan". He was probably old enough to be receiving social security as my grandmother did, but he also was a farmer. There was a chicken coop right behind his house, and across the road on his property was a small barn where he raised pigs. Further down the road he also had several rows of grapevines and cherry trees.   When I got older my first job was to pick cherries for Mr. Dickinson and I earned two cents a pound.

We went up the rickety back steps to Mr. Dickinson's kitchen and he greeted us at the door.   There was a sort of metal plate to scrape mud off of one's feet.

"Morning, Mrs. Degan" he smiled.   He tipped his cap but put it back on his head.

"Morning, Mr. Dickinson, lovely day isn't it." she smiled back.   I hung behind her apron and mumbled a "Good Morning".   The kitchen was dark and the linoleum on the floor had seen better days.

"The news isn't good about the war in Europe," my grandmother offered.

"Well, you know, we have to be careful of those '*Rooskies*'" he replied.

I knew he was referring to the Russians because I heard my grandmother say it.   I could tell from the tone of their conversation that it was serious.   While so far we were not actually in the war, England and Europe were suffering greatly. Americans had family members living in Europe and England and concern for them was growing stronger.   There was mistrust of the Russians although they were fighting against Adolph Hitler and the Nazis.   We knew nothing of the fate of the Jewish people in Poland at this time.   I don't know if Mr. Dickinson read the newspapers as consistently as my grandmother, but I believe he listened to the radio which I could hear crackling in the background.

"Jean, would you like to see the new batch of chicks I just received?" Mr. Dickinson asked.

I was startled out of my silence.   They had stopped talking about the world situation and decided to take a walk to the chicken coop.   It was nearing noon and the sun was bearing down on the backyard.   We headed out to the chicken coop in his backyard.   As soon as he opened the door I felt the rush of stifling heat.   Mr. Dickinson checked the temperature gauge.

"110 degrees..that's good…these little chicks need to be kept pretty warm the first few days."

I was melting.   Gramma kept nudging me forward into the coop and I wanted to run out of there as fast as I could.   The stench of chicken poop in the chicken coop was overwhelming.   Gramma kept smiling.

"They look like a fine batch", Gramma said to him.

Hundreds of little yellow balls were scampering all over the coop, on top of each other, over the feed boxes--everywhere. Peeping...cheeping...and scattering seed all over the sawdust on the floor, the little chicks took no mind of us.

Suddenly, Mr. Dickinson picked up one of the little yellow chicks and thrust it into my hand..

"Here, hold onto the little fella'" he said, as if this was the greatest thing he could share with me. I was terrified. The warm little body felt as if it were full of tiny bones that could break if I so much as moved my palm.

"Yeah...that's...that's....here Gramma, you can hold it." I said as I stuffed the little ball into her hand. She could tell I was terrified, and took the little chick and held it up to the light remarking on how "bright and healthy" it looked. Mr. Dickinson glowed like a father who had just given birth to this little chick.

After these chicks reached sellable age, he would put them in cartons, load them into the back of his Model T Ford and drive them off to market. I was never told what happened to them after that and I never really cared. I assumed that once they were grown up, someone else would want to buy them. Slaughter was not in my mind.

THE GORMLEYS

Grampa had also built another house on Telegraph Road in Gasport. On the other side of that road lies the Erie Barge Canal. The house was a well-constructed two story conventional structure which like many others of that era had an outside toilet. Village running water had not reached very far outside of town. I'm not sure if Grampa built the house especially for his daughter Esther and her husband Peter Gormley, but they did live there in 1940 with their five children. The oldest was Tom (named after my grandfather), twin girls Mary and Margaret, Nancy (a year or so younger than I was) and Eddie the youngest.

The family was for me the ideal one. Aunt Esther (several years older than my mother) was an excellent cook and housekeeper. I loved being invited there to visit or to stay overnight because I was assured of wonderful meals and family fun. Uncle Pete, who worked at the General Motors plant in nearby Lockport, was a fun-loving happy guy. He could play the guitar and sing and in the evenings the whole family would sit around singing. My two cousins, Margaret and Mary, would put on skits and Nancy and I would join in with our own jokes and acts. Aunt Esther would make giant bowls of hot buttered popcorn for all of us.

There were always family stories and joyful times. In his early years, Uncle Pete had been a boxer and took the name "Kid Gormley". Nancy and I would pour over yellowed newspaper clippings about Kid Gormley's fights. Nancy was very proud of her dad. On weekends, with my grandmother's permission, I would pile in their old car and we would all drive the seven miles to Lockport to the movies. There were two movie theaters in Lockport, The Rialto and The Palace. We all loved cowboy movies and went to see Roy Rogers, Dale Evans, Tom Mix and Hopalong Cassidy. Then, Nancy, Eddie, and I would come home and spend the next week pretending we were Roy Rogers, Dale Evans and others in the movie. No one wanted to be Gabby Hayes.

Since Gramma did not have a telephone, in order to contact The Gormleys we had to walk through the backyard fields and then cross the railroad tracks to reach them. The grass and weeds were up to Gramma's shoulders and over my head, but we tramped along and in about 20 minutes we had crossed the railroad tracks and were at their backyard.   Aunt Esther always seemed to have wash hanging from clotheslines in the backyard, so we made our way carefully through the white sheets and pillowcases.

"Good afternoon," Gramma shouted so as not to surprise them too much.

"Well, I'll be" responded Aunt Esther "looked what the cat dragged in."

We all laughed. Nancy came running out the back door happy to see me. Uncle Pete and Aunt Esther were quite protective of the children and would not allow them to go anywhere on their own.   They were not allowed to cross the road because of the canal on the other side and heavy traffic.

On the other hand, perhaps because I lived in Buffalo, I was able to have more independence. My parents allowed me to take the Greyhound Bus on my own from Buffalo to Gasport, about 25 miles. In Buffalo, my friends and I would take the city bus, or streetcar, to the movie theater about two miles away. Learning to do that I advanced to taking the city bus to the terminal in downtown Buffalo where I caught the bus to Gasport.

Gramma would visit with Esther and the others while Nancy and I would run out into the woods to an abandoned house which we called "Annie's" after the recluse who had lived and died there. We believed the house was haunted and would end up scaring ourselves and running back home as fast as we could. Sometimes Gramma would let me stay and other times I would have to go home with her. I enjoyed both choices.. Today was a day when I returned back across the field with Gramma. Uncle Eddie had promised to take me swimming with him to Mirror Lake.

MIRROR LAKE

There was a path at the end of our backyard that took us to the shallow end of Mirror Lake. Within 10 minutes we would come to a small waterfall that channeled water from the hills across the road to a creek that ran around the back of our house and eventually ended up in this lake.   While it was a natural body of water the railroad had enlarged it by blasting a large area to supply water for the trains that passed alongside. The owner of the property that included the lake was Arthur Shaffer. He saw the potential for a recreation area and took advantage of it by renting boats, hiring a lifeguard and charging an admittance fee. Because we were neighbors he assured my Uncle Eddie and grandparents that we would not have to pay an entrance fee. This worked out generally but as time passed, the lifeguards and workers did not recognize us as neighbors and we had to pay the 35 cents a day fee or "sneak in" which we did when we had no money.

As yet I could not swim, but Uncle Eddie would put me on his back and swim from one side of the shallow area to the other. The water was about 5 feet deep at the shallow end and only 10 or feet across to the other side. Further down, the lake widened and became over 15 or 20 feet deep and much wider. My parents laughed about it being called "Mirror Lake" since when they were growing up it was always called Shaffer's Pond--or sarcastically referred to as "the mud hole". The fact was that when the Spring floods came the water of the creek would fill our backyard just in front of the outside toilet and worked as a natural cleaner washing the contents all the way to the lake. I tried not to think about it when we went there.

UNCLE EDDIE

Uncle Eddie was the consummate bachelor. Handsome, witty and intelligent, he always seemed to have women driving him home or picking him up to go out. As far as I could tell, he was usually not the pursuer, but the pursued. On Sundays he would dress up in his white "ice cream" summer linen suit, put on his white panama hat, his shiny brown wing-tip shoes and go sauntering in a John-Wayne type of walk down the road to The Hammond Hotel. He would take me with him and after an orange soda and potato chips at the bar, I would be sent to the drugstore for the newspapers and ice cream to carry home for Gramma.

Today was Saturday and he did not have to go to work. After breakfast we were all set to go to Mirror Lake. Uncle Eddie took a bar of soap from the kitchen as he planned on "soaping down" and using the lake for a bath.

"Jean, are you ready to go? Got your bathing suit? I've got the soap for us." he beamed with his kind of wicked smile showing the gold teeth in the side of his mouth. Gramma was of course worried. I could see it in her eyes.

"You be careful with her, remember she doesn't know how to swim." Gramma pleaded.

"Don't worry, once she goes down they'll never find her." Uncle Eddie joked. The joke was funny to him, but I was never quite sure.

We walked through the bushes down the path and soon we were at the shallow end of the lake. No one was here yet. It was still early in the day for a swim and the lake wasn't opened until the lifeguards came on duty around 11 o'clock in the morning. The water was not too clear, fortunately, so I couldn't see the fish or other creatures that called this pond home.

There were white wooden steps going down into the water on both sides of the small inlet. Uncle Eddie sat on the second step and splashed water all over his body. He soaped himself into a lather and slid into the warm water. The suds soon disappeared and it was my turn. I just wanted to hang on to Uncle Eddie's neck, but he gently put my arms down and put some soap on my arms, neck and legs and dipped me into up to my neck.

"Okay, Jean, now get on my back and we'll swim to the other side." I did and it was a wonderful feeling skimming through the water. I knew I would soon learn to swim so I would be able to do what Uncle Eddie was doing as he swam arm over arm through the water.

Uncle Eddie's bathing suit had a top sleeveless part to it, sort of like an undershirt. It had red and white stripes and tucked into black trunks. In those days men did not bare their chests. At least in Gasport. We both got out of the water and sat on our towels on the grass and let the sun dry us off.

"Next time we come here, I'm going to rent a row boat and teach you how to row," Uncle Eddie remarked. I could hardly wait. I had watched others rowing around the lake and it looked wonderful. It never entered my mind that Uncle Eddie had another joke up his sleeve in an attempt to help me conquer some of my fears. He had two distinct types of laughter. One was a kind of grinning warm know-it-all laugh The other was a loud deep roaring laugh that made you want to join him even if you didn't know what was so funny.

THUNDER AND LIGHTNING STORM

That afternoon the clouds began to gather and the sky turned a steely gray. Gramma took down the wash that was hanging in the backyard and shut some of the windows. Uncle Eddie went out onto the covered front porch and sat in Gramma's rocking chair watching the wind turn the leaves upside down on the Horse Chestnut tree. Gramma always said it was going to rain when the leaves turned upside down.

"Jeanie…come on out here with me on the front porch" Uncle Eddie yelled.

"I think it's going to rain, Uncle Eddie…."

"Come on, get out here with me and let's watch the storm."

I cautiously walked out onto the front porch and he motioned for me to sit in the chair next to the rocker.

BANG! …the first bolt of lightning lit up the sky over the hills in front of us. The front porch shook and the horse chestnut tree shivered. Then a giant rumble of thunder rolled through the air and I started for the front door.

"*Get back here!*" Uncle Eddie said. "Nothing's going to hurt you."

CRACK!…CRACK! Two loud sharp clatters of lightning lit the sky up again and Uncle Eddie let out one of his deep loud laughs! I think it was right after he saw my terrorized face.

The thunder was so loud, all I could hear was Uncle Eddie's deep laugh, and see his gold teeth shining from his smiling mouth. I must have looked as if I had seen a ghost. This whole scene went on for what seemed like an hour, but it was probably less than 20 minutes. All I know is that at the end of it, I was no longer afraid of thunder and lightning, because I had begun to join Uncle Eddie in laughing every time we saw the lightning and heard the thunder. He laughed me right out of my fears. I never hear a thunder and lightning storm now without thinking of Uncle Eddie and his uproarious laugh and I smile to myself. You cured me, Uncle Eddie!

I suppose that big horse chestnut tree could have been struck and fallen over on top of us, but it never did. I have a feeling it respected Uncle Eddie also.

"Monday I'm going to have to take a load of lumber up to Tonawanda, do you want to ride with me?" Eddie asked.

"Oh, can I go Gramma?" I pleaded. She agreed.

"Yes, I want to go. What time do we have to leave?"

"Well, pretty early in the morning. I'll go into work and get the truck loaded up and then come by and pick you up."

I was wild with anticipation. Riding in the truck with Uncle Eddie all the way to Tonawanda. I wondered where Tonawanda was. It sounded far away. Probably inhabited by Indians! My imagination was writing a script already.

SUNDAY - ON THE FRONT PORCH

After I came back from The Hammond Hotel on Sunday afternoon, Gramma and I would sit on the front porch and receive visitors. Men and women would be walking along East Avenue for a Sunday stroll and many of them would stop underneath the shade of the wide leaves of the horse chestnut tree to cool off. Grampa would usually be sitting on the wooden bench under the tree and some of the men came and sat next to him to chat. Others would come up onto the front porch and chat with Gramma.

"Mornin' Mrs. Degan, fine day isn't it.," one of the men said.

"Well, after that terrible storm we had yesterday afternoon, I'm surprised it turned out so nice," replied Gramma.

Then the discussion would turn to news of the neighbors or the worsening war in Europe. I sat quietly and listened, surely not understanding how this war would soon impact our entire family.

At the very side of the road directly in front of our house, Grampa had built a concrete *stepping block*. This stepping block looked like two steps from any stairway just standing alone. When horses, or a carriage would pull up to the house, riders would use this stepping block to exit. It had been quite a few years since a carriage or horse had come down East Avenue and used this, but I delighted in it. I sat on it for hours and watched the cars go up and down the road. Sometimes I would arrange my rock collection on it and hope that passersby would stop and notice it. I wondered why no one else had a stepping block.

Because it was Sunday, Gramma said she had a feeling that my parents and little sisters would drive down to visit us. I had not seen them in a few weeks and felt some homesickness. I wondered if they had missed me or if they were just so taken with my new little sister that they didn't think about me at all. I decided to do something to test this out. Earlier in the week, I had seen someone downtown with their arm in a sling getting much attention from everyone.

"Gramma, can I use one of your kitchen towels?"

"Whatever for?"

"I want to put my arm in a sling…kind of like I had a broken arm."

"Why, you'll scare your parents half to death." she replied.

Exactly what I had in mind. Gramma went along with it and helped me put my arm in a sling. She put a big safety pin in it to hold it around my neck. The more I had my arm in the sling, the more I felt that my arm was in fact broken. I went out and sat on the stepping block and waited…and waited. I noticed that people passing by in cars were looking sadly at me also. *It felt so good!* I just might wear this all the time I thought.

After what seemed like an eternity I saw my parent's car coming slowly down the road. I put on my best forlorn face as they pulled into the driveway. As soon as my mother saw me, she looked startled. She got out of the car with my little sister, Joanne, who was a little over a year old, running alongside her. My sister Mary Ann had just been born in May and was still in a bassinet.

"What on earth happened to you?" my mother asked.

Gramma interceded and told her not to get upset. She told her I just wanted to play a joke. Actually, I wanted some attention because I felt quite jealous of all the attention my two sisters had been receiving the past year. But I wasn't able to verbalize this to her. My father got out of the car with a smile. It didn't take him long to figure out that the makeshift towel on my arm was not put there by a doctor.

He had brought my grandmother a giant jar of pickled pig's feet--one of her favorite treats. My father was a butcher and worked at a meat market in Buffalo. Then he went over under the tree to chat with Grampa. He was going to take him for a ride to the adjoining town, Middleport, to a bar called, "Tony's" and then to the cemetery where Grampa liked to visit. Grampa looked forward to these visits and he and my father got along famously. Sometimes I would get to ride along with them and maybe today would be one of those *times*.

OFF TO MIDDLEPORT

My father had parked the black two door Chevy sedan on the side of the road under the shade of the 30 ft. tall Horse Chestnut tree. While he and Grampa were sitting on the bench talking I had an idea. Maybe they wouldn't let me go with them to Middleport, but…if…I hid in the back seat of the car… I crawled on my hands and knees to the other side of the car and carefully opened the door so they wouldn't hear it. Without closing the door tight I crawled onto the floor of the backseat and waited.

It wasn't long before they piled into the two front seats and started off down East Avenue heading west towards Middleport. The floor was hard and every time we hit a bump I thought they would hear me bouncing up and down. Finally, after about 10 minutes I jumped up and said, "Hi, I thought I would go along with you."

I'm not sure to this day if they knew I was there all along, but judging by Grampa's expression, I don't think he knew. They both acted very surprised.

"Your mother's going to worry about you and blame us for not telling her you were going with us," my father said. I hadn't thought of that.

Middleport is only a few miles from Gasport and we were soon turning onto the Main Street. Tony Nicolia's grille was just across the lift bridge over the Erie Canal and the parking area was adjacent to the water. I had been there with my folks before and always froze every time we turned around in that narrow parking lot by backing right up to the edge of the water. Each time I thought I was a goner. And I wasn't even aware of the possibility that whatever they had to drink in there might have affected their perception of how close they came to the edge.

As soon as we went through the front door, the stale smell of beer and smoking filled my nostrils.

"Well, look who's here" bellowed Tony. Tony weighed at least 300 pounds, and his son Blasé who was a teenager ran a close second to his dad. They were full of smiles and greetings all around--even to me. Two glasses of beer were put up on the bar for my dad and Grampa and a glass of root beer for me. My father ordered some potato chips for me also.

"Now, Jeanie, Blasé would be a good boyfriend for you," my dad said.

Oh, no, I thought. If Blasé ever fell on me I would be crushed. I don't know if it was a joke, but I had the feeling that my dad thought it would be a definite plus being related to a bar owner. Blasé did come over and talk to me. He was a kind and generous boy with a handsome face and black curly hair. If only he could lose a hundred pounds or so I thought. My dad kept mentioning the possibilities and I wondered if I should come to Middleport anymore.

After some time we left the bar and drove to the Middleport Catholic Cemetery which was just a mile or so away. We stopped at a greenhouse just before the cemetery and my dad bought some pots of geraniums to place on the family graves. Grampa got out of the car along with my dad and they walked around the gravestones pointing out family members and former friends of my grandfathers. The cemetery felt very peaceful and I was told to be careful not to walk on people's graves which was quite a feat.

(Sunday in Gasport.   Top: Eddie Engle, Dorothy Kolb, Allan Casey
                                 Bottom: Al Kolb, D. Jean Kolb, Mary Ann Degan, Lillian Siefert
                                 Child: Joanne Kolb
                                 Jar of pickled pig's feet)

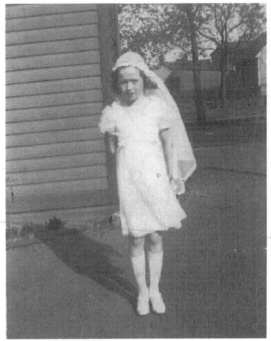

(First Communion, D. Jean Kolb.)

(Elizabeth Degan)

(Tom & Elizabeth)

We headed back to Gasport with me bumping along in the backseat looking at myself in the rearview mirror. My face had exploded with freckles this summer and my braids were loosely tied. Gramma didn't braid them as tight as my mother did and they tended to unravel all around my face and over my "Kolb ears" which I inherited from my dad.

SUNDAY VISITORS

When we pulled into the driveway, Gramma came running out to the car. "Why didn't you tell us that you were taking Jeanie with you?"

"We didn't know, she hid in the back seat of the car and popped up when we were almost to Middleport." my dad replied. She look relieved and never reprimanded me. It was enough that she was upset and I vowed never to worry her like that again. I just never even thought about the consequences--only what I wanted to do. Learning to consider the consequences of my actions was to continue to be a life long challenge.

There was another car in the driveway when we returned. My Uncle "Mirt" (Martin) his wife Marian and several of my cousins had come to visit. My Uncle Mirt was older than my mother and had several children, Bill, Bob, Virginia, Mary Jane, Delores, Richard (a year older than me) and Raymond (a year younger than me). All of them were not there, but I remember Dick (Richard) and Raymond standing under the horse chestnut tree all dressed up. I was clad in my usual shorts and summer top and tried to hide behind Gramma's apron. Sharing her with other cousins was not something I was accustomed to experiencing.

Uncle Mirt and the family lived in nearby Lockport where he worked at the local General Motors plant. From time to time Uncle Mirt would have bouts with alcoholism but Aunt Marian rarely spoke about this. She was an excellent seamstress and this added to the family income substantially. When Uncle Mirt was not drinking, he was charming and extremely intelligent. He had made many suggestions at work that earned him very good monetary rewards. But when he "fell off the wagon" as my family referred to it, he became embarrassing to himself and the family. Today he was cold sober and full of funny stories and Marian and the children looked at him with admiration.

I was fairly shy and didn't say anything to Dick or Raymond. They had on white shirts and ties and shiny oxfords. I felt like a ragamuffin. They did not stay for more than an hour and I later learned that no one wanted to have any beer or drink while Uncle Mirt was there so as not to tempt him to begin.

Sunday was a day when the family dropped in on Gramma and I can still remember the laughing and joking that went on. They teased Gramma and also made sure that she had everything she needed. My father always brought my Grandpa 100 pounds of sugar. Grampa made his own cider and was always grateful for this gift. And Gramma opened her pickled pig's feet and shared. I could hardly stand the sight of those pink feet in the big jar and no one could get me to taste them.

RIDING WITH UNCLE EDDIE

"Jean...you better get up...it's almost 9 o'clock and Eddie will be here soon to pick you up," Gramma called from the bottom of the stairs.

"Okay, Gram", as I jumped out of the big bed and went to the wash basin to dip my hands and face in the cool water, dry off and put on my shirt and pants. I could smell the bacon frying and the coffee perking. Gramma had a place set for me at the kitchen table and already had toasted me two pieces of bread that showed the black rings of the griddle on them. She took the handle for the round griddle and lifted the griddle cover up to poke the burning wood. It would be hotter by afternoon and she needed to do all her cooking in the morning, so she could let the fire go out.

I heard the big truck pull into the gravel driveway and ran to the front door. Yes, it was Uncle Eddie with a load of lumber hanging over the back of the truck.

"Come on, jump in" he said, "we've got to be in Tonawanda before noon so there will be someone there to help unload this lumber."

Gramma waved goodbye from the front porch and I leaped up onto the big front bench seat next to Uncle Eddie. He had on his baseball cap, a red and black wool shirt and jeans. There were no seat belts then so I practically had my nose right up to the front windshield of the truck trying to see everything possible. He put the gearshift into reverse and carefully backed out of the one-lane driveway. Grampa was already sitting on the bench under the horse chestnut tree watching the whole scene. He and Uncle Eddie didn't speak either.

Uncle Eddie was grinning at me as he watched what I was doing out of the corner of his eye. The truck made a groaning noise as we climbed up the first hill on East Avenue. I worried about the lumber sliding off the back of the truck because I saw that it was not tied on. Uncle Eddie assured me that he had yet to lose a load of lumber. I still worried. Soon we were on the main road heading south towards Buffalo and Tonawanda. Houses and telephone poles passed like a blur as I watched through the front window. We were really speeding south with the sun shining in the window on Uncle Eddie's hands as they lightly held the big steering wheel maneuvering us down the highway.

After about 45 minutes of bumping along, Uncle Eddie rolled down his window and put his arm out to signal a left turn off the highway into the parking area of Vohwinkle's Tavern in Millersport. I knew this place because whenever my parents drove from Buffalo to Gasport we would make this half-way stop for "refreshments". This meant a beer for the adults and root beer or orange pop for me.

"Come on, Jean, we're going to get a drink here, " Uncle Eddie said as he opened the truck door and stepped down. I jumped out of my side and joined him as we walked out of the sunshine into the dark tavern. The smell of stale beer, cigarette smoke and humidity met my keen sense of smell. It was cool and pleasant inside the tavern. We sat at a table near the bar and the bartender came over to greet Uncle Eddie whom he seemed to know very well.

"What'll it be for the little girl?"

"You can have whatever you want, Jean, are you hungry?"

"Well, I WOULD like a ...hamburger" I meekly replied. Hamburger's were just about my favorite food and my mother had nicknamed me "Wimpy".

"A hamburger it is then," said Uncle Eddie. "And how about a root beer or an orange?"

"I'll have orange pop today!"

Even though it was early for lunch, the bartender yelled into the kitchen for the cook to make me a hamburger. Uncle Eddie ordered a cool draft beer for himself. Air conditioning in trucks and cars was not yet customary, and it had been warming up inside the big truck with the engine forcing hot air through the vents. I looked admiringly at my Uncle Eddie as I chewed my giant delicious hamburger. It seemed he could do just about anything. He was in complete control.

After he finished his beer and I had devoured my hamburger and pop, I asked to use the restroom. A real indoor bathroom! It was great--even with hot running water. While I had all these things where we lived in Buffalo, when I was in Gasport it was outside toilet and cool water in the morning.

We headed out into the hot almost-noon sun and climbed back up into the lumber laden truck. Uncle Eddie eased out onto the two-lane road when there were no other vehicles in sight and the engine groaned again as he shifted the truck into high gear. Traffic was picking up now with many other cars and trucks coming and going in both directions.

"Only another half hour and we'll be at the lumberyard in Tonawanda", Uncle Eddie assured me. I really didn't care. Watching the world go by and sitting next to Uncle Eddie, I was in Heaven.

Soon I saw the lumberyard sign as Uncle Eddie shifted down to a lower gear, put his arm out the window again signaling a turn and we pulled into the long narrow opening of the yard. Uncle Eddie got out of the truck and went into the office to announce our arrival and request some men to come and start unloading the truck.

He beckoned me to get out and come into the office and wait for the unloading to be completed. Whenever Uncle Eddie was with other adults, you could hear his deep laughter and others responding to him in the same way. I wasn't sure what they were all laughing about but it sounded wonderful to me. He had a charisma and kindness that melted me along with everyone else. I didn't realize it then, but he always lived in the moment. He never voiced a worry about the future or concern about what had happened in the past. We definitely lived every moment. He took great delight in my joy of discovery, and I in his bigger- than- life presence.

Too soon we were pulling back into our driveway on East Avenue where Gramma was sitting in her rocker on the front porch with a relieved expression that I was home and safe. Uncle Eddie had to take the truck back and said he would return later. Gramma knew that "later' was much later.

SUMMER EVENING

Gramma asked me to relate the events of the day to her. I climbed up on her lap and she began to move the rocking chair back and forth. Her body was warm and I felt completely loved. I told her all about the truck ride, the traffic and stopping at Vohwinkels for a hamburger and orange pop. I knew she did not approve of Uncle Eddie having beer while he was driving the truck, not by anything she said but by her expression which I had learned to read.

The fruit on the sweet cherry tree in the side yard next to the pump was almost ripe. "These are early Richmonds" Gramma told me "and ripen near the 4th of July." I could hardly wait to taste them. The branches were low enough for Gramma to be able to pick a basket, and I had also learned how to get up into the branches of the tree and pick cherries on my own. As we went to the pump to get some cool water, Gramma reached up to one of the branches and picked a few cherries for us. I remember those plump whitish-red cherries as having the sweetest taste. Grampa had installed the pump over a natural well beneath it, so there was plenty of water for the early Richmond tree to produce juicy cherries.

I was beginning to recuperate from my long day and asked if I could comb Gramma's hair. She took the comb out of the back of her braided bun and let her silver white hair fall down around her shoulders. I took the comb and began to let it slide through her hair. There were no snarls and the comb simply swept from top to bottom. I didn't know how to style it or do much with it, just comb it until Gramma said it was time to put it back up in the braid.

We went inside for dinner and I sat at the head of the big oak table waiting for Gramma to bring my plate to me. It was ham, boiled potatoes and a dish of elderberries she had picked from the field in back of the house. And then there

was the giant cup of coffee with canned milk and sugar. After dinner we went
back out on the porch and watched the sun set down behind the hills.

"Time to climb the golden ladder," Gramma said as we made out way up
the wooden steps to our bedroom. I knew I would start the night out in Gramma's
bed at the top of the stairs, and after we said the Rosary I would be sent into the
other front bedroom where it was *healthier* to sleep by myself. I had already
concocted a list of reasons why it would be better to stay and sleep with
Gramma, but I rarely won.

"Our Father who art in Heaven…hallowed be thy name…" Gramma
began, as I followed her words and learned the Our Father and the Hail Mary.
As we prayed a train whistle sounded across the field from the rear of the house.

"That's the 9:30 train going east to Rochester", Gramma said. Trains
were close to being on time and you could almost set your clock by them according
to Gramma. I wondered how far Rochester could be and if I would ever get to go
there.

"Gramma, of all your thirteen children who did you love most?" I would
regularly ask her.

"Well, Jean, I loved all of them, but I love YOU more." she would consistently
reply. And this is exactly what I was fishing for--the ultimate prize. I wanted, like most
children to be loved *best*. The recent births of both my younger sisters after I had
been an only child for almost 7 seven years had no doubt made me insecure in my former
place.

I don't know if it was all the food I had that day--the hamburger, the orange pop,
but suddenly I had the urge to go to the bathroom. Gramma obliged, getting out of her
warm bed, putting on her robe and slippers and accompanying me down the long cool
cement sidewalk to the outhouse where she waited outside the door. I left the door
opened a crack so I could see her--and the stars.

"Look at all those stars, Gramma," I said. "They must be very far away."

"Yes, Jean, can you see the big dipper?" I really could make out the shape
of a big dipper, like we had in our kitchen.. "And there's the little dipper….the
seven sisters…" A new world of the stars opened up for me which was followed
by unending questions about God, Heaven the stars and other queries which Gramma
patiently explained to me. With two little babies, only 13 months apart, my mother
did not have the same amount of time as Gramma did to answer my unending questions.

We returned to our warm beds and another beautiful day had come to an end.

UNCLE SAM THE GROCERY MAN

"It's Wednesday, Jean, Uncle Sam is coming today," Gramma announced. Uncle Sam was not really our uncle, but a grocery delivery man who came to Gasport once a week and stopped at various houses. Gramma was on his list of stops!

The white paneled truck -- which would now resemble a large conversion van--came rolling down East Avenue, and Uncle Sam gave two "toots" on the horn to let us know he had arrived. He pulled up right in front of the stone stepping block so Gramma and I could step up on it and see into the truck. The side panel of the truck opened up to form a sort of counter where Uncle Sam could dispense his goods.

"Good morning, Mrs. Degan," Uncle Sam smiled. He was a short, baldish man and his size no doubt enabled him to walk back and forth between the shelves inside the truck selecting items.

"Good morning, Sam," replied Gramma. "I have Jean with me now so I'll be ordering more items today."

I peeked inside the van and saw shelves of bread, cakes, and canned goods. He did not have any cooler or refrigerated items. The local milkman carried milk and butter, and we got our eggs from Mr. Dickinson next door with his many chickens. Uncle Sam also had gifts and candy for sale. He had his name emblazoned on the side of the truck, "UNCLE SAM - THE GROCERY MAN". You wouldn't forget it.

I'm not sure how fresh Uncle Sam's wares were, but I do remember one instance when I had to choose my own bread from Gramma's sideboard. For some reason I cannot recall, Gramma had to go somewhere and leave me alone during lunchtime. She had left a note that there was a bowl of fresh strawberries on the kitchen table, bread was in the marble topped sideboard and peanut butter in the kitchen cupboard. I remember feeling it was quite an adventure to be left on my own for a few hours. The first thing I did was begin to eat the strawberries right out of the big bowl. Gramma would have died to see me with a big spoon just gulping away. I finished the entire bowl! Later I became quite ill and to this day do not enjoy the sweet taste of strawberries. My lesson in gluttony.

Next I went to the sideboard for two slices of bread. I noticed that some of the bread in the rear of the cupboard had a greenish tint to it. This looked absolutely intriguing to me. Where had Gramma ever bought green bread? Must be a special from Uncle Sam, so I chose the pieces with the most green on them. I spread them with peanut butter and took an enormous bite of the sandwich. By the time the moldy taste had become apparent to me, I was gagging uncontrollably. I had discovered what moldy bread looked like! It seems that despite Gramma's trust in me I had failed miserably. First the strawberries and now the moldy bread. Learning the hard way, but lessons never to be forgotten.

Uncle Sam and Gramma spent quite a bit of time chatting while I walked around the truck. Finally, Uncle Sam asked if I would like to get inside the truck. Yes. He lifted me in and I walked up and down the aisles amazed at all the food he had managed to stuff inside that little truck. I thought this might be a very interesting job to have in the future. I could be "Aunt Jean…the grocery girl?" Didn't sound right.

Uncle Sam finally pulled away and headed for the next house down the street. Gramma and I went back into the house to put away all our groceries. I'm not sure where Gramma got her money. I suppose Social Security and no doubt Uncle Eddie and Uncle Emmett gave her some money for food. The cost of electricity was minimal and we had plenty of wood for the cook stove. The furnace in the basement was fed with coal or wood, but in the spring, or whenever there was consistent rain, water covered the cement floor and sometimes rose high enough to put out the fire. Then we all huddled in front of the cook stove in the kitchen to keep warm. But this was summer and that was enough heat for us.

AUNT HELEN (DEGAN) CASEY

Aunt Helen was a few years younger than my mother but as different in personality as possible. Whereas my mother was quiet, friendly and unassuming, Aunt Helen was a firecracker! She had bright red (strawberry blonde) hair with a temperament to match. And she married Uncle Al Casey almost 10 years her senior, so we always thought the song "Casey Would Waltz With The Strawberry Blonde" was written for them. Like most of the Degan women she was just over 5 feet tall, but with beautiful facial features, high cheekbones and the big translucent blue "Degan eyes". All the siblings had the *Degan eyes*. Even in my own family where my father had brown eyes--which should dominate--all of us girls had the *"Degan eyes."*

Aunt Helen's had a sparkle to them, like tiny firecrackers were exploding all the time. She was full of plans, ideas and adventures. It was like a whirlwind when she would fly into the house and Gramma would just sit back and watch it happen. Aunt Helen smoked and spent time at the local pub, "The Hammond Hotel", along with her brothers and friends.

"Al and I are here to take Jeanie to the circus, Ma", Aunt Helen announced as she clicked through the house with her spike heels and stockings with the dark seams outlined up the back of her legs. I was beside myself with excitement having never been to a real live circus. I jumped up onto my 6' tall Uncle Al's lap and he held on to me as he asked if I wanted to go. "Do I want to GO?" I sputtered. "Gramma, can I?... Can I?..." Gramma knew it was no good to protest with Aunt Helen, so she just nodded. Gramma did not approve of Aunt Helen smoking, drinking, going to bars and I knew she was aware that I would be party to all of this. Aunt Helen went through the few clothes I had brought from Buffalo and picked out an outfit. She combed my hair so I looked like a girl instead of the way I had been wearing it. Uncle Eddie had taken me to the barbershop with him and got me a "boyish bob" which made me not only look like a boy but accented my *Kolb ears*. I had been endowed with my father's large ears instead of the dainty Degan ears.

Uncle Al and Aunt Helen had a big green Hudson sedan with a little gear shift on the steering wheel that fascinated me because I knew I could operate it if only they let me. Within a few minutes I was sitting in the back seat of the car as they backed out of the driveway waving to Gramma as she sat in her rocker on the front porch fearing the worst. We had to drive all the way to Buffalo to get to the circus and I knew we would probably stop off later at my house to visit. Aunt Helen and Uncle Al lived in Lockport and I also would spend time staying there during the summers. They lived in a downstairs flat and upstairs was a young girl my age that I could play with.

"You're going to see real elephants, tigers and men and women flying through the air on trapezes," Aunt Helen announced. Wow. I wasn't excited enough just

(Wedding: Left to right: Allan Casey, Tom & Margaret Gormley, Helen Casey)

(Parents' Wedding: Top: Edwin Degan, Al Kolb; Bottom: Ruth Kolb, Dorothy Degan)

hearing the word "circus". Aunt Helen and Uncle Al did not have any children of their own and they treated me as if I were theirs. I loved it. Once again I was an ONLY child!

Soon we were driving down a crowded street where I could see large brown tents and many cars parked in a grassy lot. Uncle Al pulled the car into one of the entrances on the grassy parking area.

"Al, I have my high heels on….how am I going to go through all this mud," Aunt Helen commented. Uncle Al said nothing. We got out of the car and began to trek towards the big tent. All of a sudden I heard Aunt Helen let out a yell. "Jesus H. Christ, Al, I just stepped in a pile of elephant shit!" Thank God Gramma didn't hear this. Sure enough her strapless high heels were soaked in what definitely smelled like elephant droppings. Uncle Al took some grass and tried to wipe off her shoe, but she was sputtering like a fire. Uncle Al was laughing and I was only intent on getting inside that big tent.

UNCLE AL CASEY

Uncle Al was tall -- and looked even taller next to Aunt Helen's 5 feet. He was 6 feet at least with black wavy hair and the beginning of a receding hair line. His large brown eyes and warm friendly manner would melt anyone. He was college educated and his book case was full of chemistry, biology and philosophy books. Whenever he gave me any advice I was all ears--Kolb ears! Mostly I remember climbing on his lap, him carrying me out to the car when I would fall asleep before they were ready to leave and all the hugs and touches that I did not receive from my own father. I understood that my father was not an openly affectionate person but that he did love me. Uncle Al more than made up for it.

THE CIRCUS

I wasn't disappointed. Everything was going on at once. There were three rings inside the tent and one had a man with a long black whip cracking it in the face of several large tigers who were sitting on top of inverted drums. The tigers growled loudly whenever he snapped his whip. In another ring there were trapeze artists flying through the air and barely catching the hands of their fellow flyers. Clowns were everywhere parading around the outer ring. I didn't know where to look…I wanted to see it all…at the same time. Uncle Al handed me a bag of popcorn and some orange soda in a paper cup. Was this living, or what! The noise was deafening with different music going on in
each ring area. I looked at Aunt Helen and could tell she was on the verge of boredom. She absorbed things quickly and was ready to move on. We stayed until the elephants finished their dance and parade and headed out to visit my parents. Maybe I could pick up some more of my clothes while I was there because I was definitely running low on outfits.

Aunt Helen suggested that I could stay with them in Lockport for the night so I didn't disturb Gramma coming home so late. This was good. Inside plumbing...a warm bath and a chance to see what was in Aunt Helen's bathroom in the way of cosmetics--shampoo, creams, etc. I wanted to look like Aunt Helen when I grew up and be glamorous and vivacious. I also wanted to be like Uncle Al who played the trombone in a marching band at the General Motors Company - Harrison Radiator - where he worked. When I stayed at their apartment, Aunt Helen let me put on his marching band hat and I would march around the house saluting and pretending to be Uncle Al. She kept the hat in the side door of her buffet, and as soon as he went off to work, I headed for the buffet.

Aunt Helen kept a spotless house. The floors were always shiny, and you could see your face in the dining room table it was waxed so much. It didn't seem to take her any time at all to have the house in order, and by the time Uncle Al came home, she would have a delicious dinner prepared. They had lots of friends and they took me along on their picnics and parties so I got to hear all kinds of grown-up conversation which I devoured. But I missed Gramma and thought of her all alone in her rocking chair on the front porch while I was having such a great time.

STOPPING AT 56 KEPPEL STREET

As we left the tent Aunt Helen insisted that Uncle Al go to the parking area alone and pick her up at the curb. No more elephant surprises on her shoes. I waited with her as Uncle Al drove up to the curb and picked us up. We headed towards my parent's house which was only a few miles away in South Buffalo. They wanted to see how the babies were doing--my sister Joanne who turned one year old in April, and my newest sister, Mary Ann who was born prematurely on May 24th of this year, 1940. I remembered when Joanne was born at the hospital and I was not allowed to go in to see her. Aunt Helen told me not to worry that I could wait in the car in the parking lot and she would hold Joanne out the window so I could see her. Leave it to Aunt Helen to fix things. I did wait outside in the parking lot next to the car, and when I looked up to what was the 7th or 8th floor of Buffalo General Hospital, I saw my Aunt Helen holding a big white bundle out of the hospital window and waving to me. I couldn't really make out the baby because it was so far away but I felt thrilled that I had "seen" the baby. In later years I found out that she only held out a big white pillow.

I have to admit being quite jealous of the new baby and all the attention she was getting from everybody. No longer the only child I sunk into the background and found solace in Gramma and the Degan clan. Because Joanne was a healthy large baby, the doctor insisted she needed only Carnation canned milk which had more nutrients (fat) in it, so I was enlisted to walk to a store several blocks away where it was available. I did feel good about being able to help but, other than this gesture, I did not help my mother with Joanne. She received a great deal of attention from the rest of the family-- especially my father who was convinced she was a "Kolb".

Mary Ann was born at home because there wasn't time to get my mother to the hospital. I remember my father carrying her up to their bedroom on the 2nd floor as Dr. Shields came running behind them. Mary Ann weighed in at a little over 5 pounds and I got to see her right away. No pillow out the window this time!

After we pulled into the driveway at my parent's home, Aunt Helen and Uncle Al went in and gushed over both the babies. By this time Joanne was a pudgy little toddler running around underfoot with light brown curly hair, and Mary Ann at three months was still in her bassinet. While I went up to my room to find some more clothes, the grownups sat around the kitchen table discussing the latest news of the war in Europe and England. There was beginning to be quite a bit of anti-German feeling in the United States, and because my father was of German ancestry that included us.

My paternal grandparents passed away before I was born so I never knew them. They emigrated from Alsace-Lorraine because of religious persecution of Catholics there by the German Lutherans, I was told. A butcher by trade, my grandfather John Kolb and his wife Mary, owned and operated Kolb's Butcher Shop in North East Buffalo for many years. They had five children, three boys and two girls. All the boys were taught the trade of meat cutting, and after their parents died the meat market was closed and my father went to work at other meat markets in Buffalo. My mother met him in Buffalo where she went to live with my Aunt Grace and Uncle Jay Yerge to find a job. They dated for seven years before they finally married.

The house where we lived now in 1940 was a small cottage behind a local tavern. There was a good-sized parking area behind the tavern that separated our house from the tavern. Next to our house was a three-car garage for the owners of the bar who lived in the house next to the bar. It was sort of a corner complex of buildings. Our small house had a kitchen, bathroom, living and dining room downstairs. Upstairs were three bedrooms, one for my parents, one for my two sisters and my own room facing Keppel Street. There was also a washing room off the dining room where my mother spent hours with diapers and baby things washing and wringing them out. We didn't have a dryer so she hung the clothes on lines strung up between our house and the three-car garage. The area was all gravel with no grass, and because there was a chemical plant nearby, National Aniline, our wash suffered. No matter how white it was when it came out of the washer, by the time my mother took it down off the line it had turned gray.

The bar was called "Hehir's" (pronounced "Hairs") after the owners, Bridget and Matt. They had one son and one daughter. Their son had recently gone to Canada to enlist in the Royal Air Force so he could fight the Germans. We were not yet in the war and he felt it his duty to defend freedom. Unfortunately he was killed early on in the war while flying a plane in England. Besides working at a meat market, my father also worked part time as a bartender at Hehir's and I could go into the back entrance, ring the buzzer on the wall and he would come and bring me a glass of pop or potato chips. On a particular hard day for my mother she would send me over to get her two bottles of beer. That was usually wash day!

The discussion about the war had become quite heated as my parents and aunt and uncle had various opinions. My father was an avid newspaper reader, as my grandmother was, and he knew what was going on in the world. Aunt Helen had her opinions regardless of the facts. Adding fuel to the fire, they had been consuming several beers. Soon my Uncle Al, the peacemaker, decided it was time to start off for Lockport. I said goodbye to my parents and we headed out. I still had another month of vacation in the country before school started in Buffalo.

ROWING ON MIRROR LAKE

It was Sunday and Uncle Eddie was going to take me in a row boat. My first time. After lunch we walked through the backyard and along the path to the shallow end of Mirror Lake. We followed along a path that led us to the main entrance where the lake fanned out to about 1/4 of a mile wide. Uncle Eddie went up to the desk to rent a row boat and Art Shaffer, the owner, saw him.

"Ed Degan...haven't seen you in a long time," Art said.

"Yes, I'm going to rent one of your row boats and teach my niece how to row."

"It's on me, Ed, you don't have to pay the rental fee," Art replied.

The young girl behind the counter gave Uncle Eddie a set of green oars and we walked down to the shore and got into the green row boat. It kind of wobbled from side to side so I sat down quickly. Uncle Eddie put the oars into the silver handles and started slicing them through the still water. We were moving! He rowed out past the middle of the lake and then edged the boat right up to the deep runoff.

"Uncle Eddie! We're going to go over the side...let's get out of here." I shrieked.

He began his deep roaring laugh and watched the panic set in on my face. I believe he was purposely trying to help me conquer some of my fears. It wasn't working. The boat kept bumping up along the 1 or 2 inch ledge around the deep well and I could see the green water swirling around and disappearing down the hole and envisioning that the two of us and the rowboat would soon be heading down this waterfall. After what seemed like a lifetime, but was actually about 3 or 4 minutes, Uncle Eddie rowed away from the waterfall.

"Okay, Jean, your turn to row, take hold of these oars and just dip them in the water and pull back."

I grabbed the heavy oars and they slid effortlessly into the water. I realized that I was heading toward the shore.

"How do I turn this around?" I asked.

"Just put one oar in the water... row and you will turn. Right oar if you want to go left, and left oar if you want to turn right," Uncle Eddie instructed.

Well, that was pretty easy I thought. I rowed all around the lake being careful to avoid the swimmers and other boaters. I felt quite proud that I had learned to row, even though it was not difficult. Uncle Eddie took the oars and maneuvered us back to the shore and helped me out.

"How would you like some ice cream?" Uncle Eddie asked.

"Yes...yes...chocolate." I replied.

He went up to the tent-covered office and came back with two big ice cream cones for us, and we sat on a picnic bench eating and watching the other boaters and swimmers. I didn't want summer to end.

THE PANCAKE LESSON

It was another summer Sunday and the temperature was climbing over the 80's. My parents and sisters had driven down from Buffalo for the day and I was enjoying myself by improving my tree-climbing skills. There was the gigantic horse chestnut tree in the front yard with strong heavy limbs that were slightly above my ability to reach. But the front yard cherry tree was perfect to climb, and I could sit up on the lower branches and watch the cars and people come and go, not to mention nibbling on the dark sweet red cherries.

I started thinking of cherry pie and then PANCAKES. The urge for pancakes with sweet maple sugar began dancing around in my head. "Gramma... Gramma... can you make me some pancakes?" I yelled as I ran through the front door to the kitchen. She and my mother were sitting at the kitchen table and my mother gave me a look that could kill.

"Jean, do you realize that the temperature is over 80 and your grandmother will have to start this cook stove going?" my mother exclaimed.

I hadn't thought about that, and at the moment I didn't care. My grandmother never said a word but started opening the griddle and putting wood into the stove to start a fire. My mother was sizzling and could have started the fire by just putting her finger on the wood. Gramma saw it too. "Dorothy, it will only take a few minutes and she really wants pancakes." I was winning. I sat at the kitchen table and watched my mother's disapproving expression and my grandmother heating up the kitchen and stirring the pancake batter. It wasn't long before I noticed the beads of sweat on Gramma's face which had begun to turn red with the heat. A stirring of conscience was beginning to grow within me. By the time the pancakes were done and on my plate, I had lost my appetite, but I did eat them slowly and thanked Gramma several times in a weak voice. My mother was right. But Gramma taught me a lesson without ever uttering a word. She let me see the results of my selfish desire, and that was enough for me.

I have never forgotten the ordeal and know that it made me think about the consequences of my wishes on those that I loved. I also know that if my mother hadn't pointed it out to me ahead of time, I might not have been so aware of it. That was one of the differences between my mother's parenting and Gramma's. Gramma never yelled--never reprimanded--only quietly corrected me when she needed to, and I never forgot the few times she did suggest a better way, or a better word. I would have done anything in my power to please her and not to do anything wrong.

THE HOUSE THAT GRAMPA BUILT

Grampa had thought of everything it seems when he built the house on East Avenue. Between the kitchen and the dining room were floor-to-ceiling wooden cabinets. The cabinets extended half the length of the rectangular-shaped kitchen. The neat thing about them was that there were doors on both sides, so if you opened the doors on both sides you could see right into the dining room. Or, in Gramma's case she could reach in and set the table from the dining room side, and when she washed and returned the dishes, it could be done from the kitchen side. For myself and my cousins it meant we could leave the cupboard doors open a crack and listen in on all the adult conversation and giggle about what they were saying.

On the bottom cabinets Gramma kept pots and pans and on the top shelves were dishes and packaged foods. She could fill the sugar bowl or the salt and pepper shakers from the dining room. With thirteen children I'm sure this saved many a step.

I remember a particular incident being held by Gramma while she reached into the cupboard to get the butter. I had been watching her iron clothes with an iron that

(Horse Chestnut Tree and Degan Home, East Avenue, Gasport)

(Hotel Hammond and Jones Drug Store - Gasport, NY)

she heated on the cookstove. In order to test whether it was ready she would lick her finger and swiftly touch it to the bottom of the iron to see if it was ready. When she left the kitchen for a moment I tried to copy what she had done. But I got it wrong. I picked up the iron and put my tongue on it. Heaven knows how I could have been that mixed up. I know I was small enough to be held by my tiny grandmother, and she insisted on slathering my tongue with butter--which I detested. The butter was worse than

the burn but finally the pain subsided. That was before ice was found to be the best antidote. Anyway, we never had ice cubes. In the summer the ice man would come carrying a giant slab of melting ice on his shoulder with a large black scissor-type tool. He would insert it into the top of the ice box and we would be set until the next day. If I remember correctly the ice cost about a penny a pound.

Near the end of the fall season my grandfather would install wood paneling around the front and back porches. It served to keep the house warmer, but it made the front and back porch dark and dreary and I longed for the Spring to come so those boards could be removed and we would once again sit in the rockers and wicker porch furniture.

The most impressive feature of the house was the giant horse chestnut tree that still sits in front of the house. Now it almost totally blocks the front of the house. My grandfather I am told brought the seedling with him from England, and through the years shaped and nurtured it. People would stop their cars to admire it and ask if they could take photos. This always made my grandfather swell with pride about his tree. The blossoms of this horse chestnut were incredibly beautiful, tall cone-shaped flowers that strangely enough despite their beauty had no smell at all. When fall came the green-spiked balls would fall from the tree and out would pop the brown horse chestnuts. You couldn't eat them, but we did make necklaces from them and threw them at each other and across the road and whatever else children could think of. I would gather bags full of them which probably helped keep the yard clean. Gramma, I believe, saw them as a messy part of the tree but never once said a word, only a warning not to throw them and hurt anyone or break any windows.

The tree provided an enormous amount of shade the leaves being very large and also cone-shaped. In the hot weather my Uncle Eddie would spread a blanket underneath the tree to lie down and I would join him. When I say "join" him, I mean I would crawl all over him--on top of his chest, on his head like a spider. He never complained and also let me comb his rather thinning brown hair as he tried to rest. My father or mother were not openly affectionate so I delighted in this touching I gave and received in Gasport. Every time Uncle Emmett saw me, it was an excuse to pick me up and throw me into the air and catch me just before I hit the floor. Gramma went nuts.

THE "SITTING ROOM"

We called it a "living room" at my house, but Gramma called it the sitting room. It opened onto the front porch through a heavy oak door that was mostly left open in the summer. There was a rather large picture window on the side facing Mr. Dickinson's house and the Richmond Cherry tree. The window did not go down to the floor as they do nowadays, but stopped about 2 feet from the floor. In front of the picture window was an oak table with a Tiffany-type lamp with a glass translucent shade that had a various colored painting all around. It was a scene of a carriage with several horses trotting through the countryside. There were also beads that hung from it. I would stare at it for long periods of time when the light was on.

Next to the table was an overstuffed chair which usually had as its inhabitant Grampa who would most always be smoking his pipe. On one side of the table he had a tray with his Prince Albert tobacco and various pipe cleaning instruments. He usually sat there with his bowler hat on and in his socks if his knee boots were muddy. Rings of smoke would encircle his hat as he quietly sat there reading the newspaper or just staring out the window. One of Grampa's eyelids sort of hung down, and while I wasn't aware of it at the time, many of us inherited what has now become known in the family as "the hanging Degan eye". Yes, I have it, and am careful to try and conceal it at any "photo shoot"! One of my second cousins actually exercises her lid thinking she may prevent the inevitability of gravity and age.

Across from the picture window on the opposite wall hung a large painting entitled "Ruins on the Rhine" and showed a castle along the Rhine River. Apparently I stared at it more than I realized because I have spent years searching for it. It was taken by my Aunt Esther years later and we do not know where it now hangs. Over the years I have collected three other "paintings on glass" that are similar. Painting on glass, that is they were painted in reverse, covered with wood or cardboard, and then framed. They were painted during the late 19th or early twentieth century, mostly by stay-at-home women. I am told they are not particularly valuable unless one likes that type of painting--which I do for sentimental reasons.

Next to the front door of the sitting room was a black mahogany upright Baldwin piano upon which I would plunk out melodies with one finger until Gramma would find a reason for us to "go visiting." I never played it when Grampa was in the house. Somehow I knew he would not like it and I had a quiet fear of him. Probably because he said very little and only seemed to smile when my dad was there with him.

The piano had been bought originally for my Aunt Helen who could play it. She very seldom had time now unless I begged her to do it. Our next door neighbor, Mr. Dickinson's son, Glenn was a piano whiz. He never took piano lessons and yet he could play anything requested. On weekends, I would see Glenn go out of the

house wearing a black suit with a white shirt and bow tie. He played the piano at
a local bar and became well known for his artistry in the area. Neither had I ever
had lessons but try as I may I could hardly ever advance from my one finger plucking
except to play "Chopsticks" which Aunt Helen taught me.

On the other side of the sitting room was a wall creating a hallway between it
and the staircase going either up to the second floor or through a doorway down
into the dank basement. Playing hide-and-go-seek in this house was Heaven! Except
I rarely had anyone with whom to play.   Besides walking up to the drugstore for the
newspapers and post office for the mail, I spent some time going up to the small
bridge over the creek.   I would sit on the stone railing and watch the water bugs skim
across the clear liquid. This is the creek that empties into Mirror Lake. I have a
beautiful photograph that I took of this scene hanging now in my home, and whenever
I see it memories flood over me of those quiet and wonderful summer days I spent
sitting on the cold stone railing looking down on life in the creek. While now and again
I did feel a twinge of homesickness for my parents, there was so much to do and see in
the country that I soon forgot these "twinges".

SUMMER OF 1940 COMING TO AN END

It had been a great summer and I had learned many things. Climbing trees,
being able to open the combination lock post office box to retrieve the mail, and
how to row. Learning to swim was still in the future. Now it was time to return
to Buffalo and third grade. Third grade held a big surprise for me because Public
School 26 had growing pains. There were too many children in the third grade and
we all had to take a test to see which two would advance to fourth grade skipping
third grade entirely. It sounded like a great idea to me and it turned out that Richard
Schwartz and I got the highest grade and were swiftly moved up to fourth grade.
I was still fairly tiny for my age and remember swimming in that big fourth grade
desk. Skipping this grade resulted in almost always being the shortest and smallest
in my class--even to high school graduation which occurred when I was only 16 years
old. In any event the next summer of 1941 brought many new world events that would
impact greatly on The Degans.

Our principal at Public School #26 was Mrs. Borrell. She was a short lady with
grayish brown curly hair that looked as if it was glued to the sides of her head. Every one
of the students, including myself, were deathly afraid of Mrs. Borrell because she had

shown us all the paddle that hung on the wall in her office. We did know of one young boy who had suffered being paddled and that kept us on our toes. Actually, I never misbehaved in school because the thought of my mother coming to school was what terrified me more than Mrs. Borrell. When I told my mother about the paddle she said, "If any teacher or principal ever lays a hand on you, I will come down to that school and wipe the floor up with them." Oh! Oh!

I was however called to Mrs. Borrell's office on several occasions, all of which duly terrified me. Because my parents would often take us to Gasport for the weekend and we would get home late on Sunday evening, I often missed school on Mondays. My mother always wrote an excuse saying I was ill. Mrs. Borrell didn't fall for that.

"Jean, now tell me just WHY is it that you seem only to be sick on Mondays? Do you have a standing Monday appointment, or what?"

I froze and insisted that I just happened to be ill on Mondays. She couldn't pull another word out of me. Many times I dragged myself to school on Mondays with only a few hours of sleep after a weekend in Gasport just so I wouldn't have to face Mrs. Borrell.

HAROLD

After returning from New Jersey the summer went by quickly. The cherry trees ripened and I continued to climb up into them--not only to eat the ripe cherries but to watch the scene below. From the highest limb I dared to climb, I would perch myself in a crotch where two sturdy limbs gave me support. I was high enough so Harold couldn't reach me.

Harold was about 40 years old, physically, with short cropped gray hair. I could see him coming down East Avenue every day with his sort of galloping walk. He walked as though he had springs in his shoes and his long legs enabled him to take great strides. Gramma confided in me that "Harold isn't quite right." Yet Gramma treated him with the same respect and welcome as she did everyone else. I was deathly afraid of Harold anyway. His small brown eyes glowed and his speech was a sort of a high-pitched sing-song. He always said the same thing. "How are YOU today?" and Gramma always replied, "Just fine, Harold, and how are you."

His face lit up and a broad weird sort of smile would appear. Then he would turn to me. "And how are YOU today?" "Umm...okay.." I would reply and run behind Gramma's apron. Sometimes he would just stand in the front yard for a few minutes, say goodbye and lope off. But if Gramma was in the kitchen he would go in there to see her. I couldn't wait until he left. This was the first person I ever knew that "wasn't quite right."

Gramma said he came from a fine family and these things just happen. He was always clean and well dressed. It was just that WALK that said it all. And since I had been perfecting my imitations of people, I learned how to do a pretty good "Harold." Gramma did not really approve of my imitations and considered them, I believe, making fun of people. Harold didn't stop at other houses as far as I could tell from my lookout perch up in the cherry tree. And I never saw Grampa talk to Harold.

DECEMBER 7, 1941

It was a Sunday and my parents, two sisters and I were spending the weekend at Gramma's. We seldom had the old radio turned on because it crackled and was full of static, so we did not know what had happened until our next door neighbor, Helen (Genet) Schultz saw us in the backyard. Gram was walking me out to the frigid outside toilet and Helen was in the backyard still in her red chenille bathrobe. She called over, "Mrs. Degan, did you hear the news? The Japanese attacked Pearl Harbor."

Gramma was silent and we hurried back into the house to spread the news. My father tried to tune the radio in with all its crackling and I think we did hear some news. My Aunt Helen and Uncle Al arrived shortly thereafter and everyone was abuzz. There was much discussion about just exactly WHERE Pearl Harbor was located. Aunt Helen, in her inimitable fashion insisted it was in New York City harbor. My mother disagreed and said it was no doubt nearer Japan. Even I was consulted but I hadn't had World Geography yet and didn't know either. Uncle Eddie said Aunt Helen didn't know what she was talking about.

Finally, President Franklin D. Roosevelt came on the radio informing us that the United States had officially entered World War II against the Axis powers, Japan, Germany and Italy. We were at war! The family discussions continued far into the night. Gramma was visibly moved. She had already lost a son, William, in World War I and her thoughts were with her youngest son, Emmett who could be drafted. As it turned out Emmett enlisted in the army soon after that and Gramma was never the same. A sadness was always in her eyes and a far-away look.

EMMETT LEAVES FOR THE ARMY

It was for me the beginning of my joy in writing. When I was at home in Buffalo, I wrote Uncle Emmett long letters and he responded. I wrote to him at Fort Dix, then to Fort Riley, Kansas and finally overseas to Europe. When I was in Gasport in the summer and other school vacations, Gramma dictated long letters to me for Emmett. Gramma could write very well but she preferred to dictate to me. We told Emmett everything and he wrote to us in kind. We lived for the mail!

Now the daily trip to town for newspapers and mail had a greater meaning. Word on the war and Uncle Emmett. When I would go inside the post office door, I could look into our glass-front box and see the red and white striped air mail envelopes and my heart would leap. I knew it was from Emmett and that Gramma would be pleased. We poured over each letter and devoured every detail.

The Allies--United States, Great Britain and Russia were not doing very well in the beginning in 1942 and 1943. We had to divide our forces between two continents, Europe and Asia. Germany had occupied France plus parts of Italy and was bombing England on a daily basis. At home there were air raid drills to prepare us for a possible invasion. My father was an air-raid warden and was given a big white metal helmet which I would don whenever he wasn't there and march around the house giving orders.

At Public School 26 in Buffalo, we also had air raid drills. A bell would ring and we all had to go out into the halls and cover our heads. Believe me, we were scared and could almost conjure up the sounds of enemy planes overhead. Many items were rationed, such as butter, sugar, coffee, meat and shoes. Each person in the family was given a ration book. There were also small red coins about the size of a dime for butter and coffee. Of course, Aunt Helen, who probably already owned twenty or thirty pairs of shoes did not despair. She went to the Ration Board and managed to get a ration book for every one of Gramma's 13 children--several of whom were no longer alive. She even got a ration book for Uncle Tommy who lived in New Jersey. Gramma was sure they would catch her and she would wind up in jail. But it didn't happen. Aunt Helen was friendly with every sheriff and authority figure in the county.

One thing she couldn't control was Uncle Al's future. At 39 years old he was drafted into the army and was sent to the Philippines. Uncle Al had a college degree and was not in the cavalry/infantry such as Uncle Emmett. We found out later that Uncle Emmett was stationed in France and his outfit was Reconnaissance. And I learned how to spell it. Meanwhile Uncle Al was on a ship bound for the South Sea Islands. I don't remember ever writing to Uncle Al.

Gramma poured over the newspapers every day and dreaded reading the names of local servicemen who had been killed or wounded. Uncle Emmett sent me home colored patches which I sewed on my blouses and jackets and proudly wore to school as other students did also.

EMMETT COMES HOME ON LEAVE

Before he was shipped overseas, Emmett came home on a ten day leave. It was a warm summer day and I had not yet packed to go to Gasport for summer vacation. All of a sudden I looked towards the kitchen doorway and

(Private First Class Emmett J. Degan, 1944)

(Top Left: Mary Ann & Joanne Kolb - 1949)(Top Right: Judy - 1948)(Bottom Left: Three friends & Joanne Kolb on far right)(Bottom Right: Ed Degan - 1951)

Uncle Emmett was standing there in full uniform. He had on the typical brown colored pants, shirt and U. S. Army cap. I almost passed out. Here he was--in the flesh. I ran up to him and even though I had grown since seeing him last he lifted me high up in the air and spun me around. My mother was very pleased to see him. He had managed to get the train to Buffalo and had a ride to our home in South Buffalo.

"Okay, Jeanie, we're going to Gasport on the bus. I don't know how to get downtown from here but I know you do." I was actually going to accompany Uncle Emmett on the bus all the way to Gasport. After he had some lunch and played with my two little sisters, he was ready to go. I packed a small suitcase and we headed down Seneca Street.

"We have to go to the corner of Bailey Avenue and take the bus all the way to Main Street near the University of Buffalo. We can catch the Greyhound bus on that corner," I said.

"Wow...I'm impressed. You'll have to show me the way. How much does it cost to ride the bus?" he added. I felt so important.

I remember boarding the bus and all eyes turned towards Uncle Emmett in his army outfit. Everyone smiled at him and I sat next to him on the bumpy bus as proud as I could possibly be. Gramma would be totally shocked seeing us walking down East Avenue together. She didn't have a phone so there was no way to alert her. Better yet.

The bus only took about 20 minutes from Seneca Street to Main Street. It would have been faster, but it stopped at almost every intersection to take on new passengers--all of whom turned their gazes to Uncle Emmett. We got off at the corner on Main Street and before long the Greyhound bus appeared and we were on our way to Gasport. The bus driver didn't tease Uncle Emmett about going to "Gas....port" the way he did to me. Again, all eyes on the bus zeroed in on us. I could have burst with pride.

In about a half-hour the bus pulled up in front of Joneses' Drug Store and we got off. Everyone we saw knew Uncle Emmett and he stopped to talk with each of them. I kept tugging on his sleeve to hurry up because I wanted Gramma to have the surprise. We briefly went into The Hammond Hotel where I had an orange pop, went to the bathroom and Uncle Emmett had a beer. The bartender would not take his money and the rest of the patrons wanted to buy him more drinks, but he said, "No thanks."

We seemed to fly down the short mile walk on East Avenue and I could see the horse chestnut tree from atop the hill. As we rounded the driveway I saw Gramma sitting in her rocker on the front porch. She did a double-take when she saw the uniform and almost leaped off the front porch. Uncle Emmett picked her up in the air as easily as he did me and spun her around in the air.

"My goodness, put me down, you'll hurt yourself," Gramma exclaimed while obviously loving every minute of it.

The three of us sat on the front porch and talked and talked and talked. Grampa came home after awhile and shook hands with Emmett and I could see the pride on his face. He wanted to know everything about the army and where they might send him. Uncle Emmett wasn't allowed to disclose where he might be sent next. We weren't sure if it would be the Pacific front or Europe. Either one was dangerous. I think that Gramma believed that this was the last time she would see Emmett alive. I was sure he was invincible.

The days went by fast. Emmett went out with his friends a few times and Aunt Helen and Uncle Al took him out also. He managed to see all of the family. My parents came down on the weekend and we were all happily together. All the Gormleys came over also to be with us all. Laughter and beer filled the house and we couldn't get enough of Emmett or his army news. When it was time for him to leave there was many tears from everyone--especially Gramma. Aunt Helen and Uncle Al drove him to Buffalo to take the train.

THE WAR CONTINUES

We continued writing letters back and forth to Uncle Emmett. Seventy thousand British civilians had been killed by German bombs, but the tide of war began to turn as Russia held back the German invasion of Stalingrad by 1943. The bitter Russian winter had been partly responsible for the German defeat. Judging from our letters, Uncle Emmett was definitely near the front lines, if not in front of the front lines because of his reconnaissance duty. Uncle Al was still alive and as far as we could tell was not in actual combat in the Pacific. Island by island, Guadalcanal, Iwo Jima, etc. the U. S. was regaining control from the Japanese.

Gramma and Mr. Dickinson discussed the possibility of Jewish men, women and children being imprisoned by the Germans in Poland, but I never heard of Jewish people being killed. I did not play close attention to their war discussions, but was more interested in family news of the Dickinson's. It seems that Mr. Dickinson did farm business with a man who lived on Upper Mountain Road named Harry Hill--a widower. Harry Hill had an unmarried daughter, Margie, who had an out-of-wedlock son named Donnie about 5 or 6 years old. Living in Mr. Dickinson's house was his unmarried, middle-aged sister Fanny, a rather quiet and strange woman, and Glenn (the pianist), his son. Mr. Hill's visit to the home lead to a romantic interest in Fanny. Ironically, Glenn fell in love with Margie and we would often hear him playing "My Little Margie" on his piano. Gramma never made any comments to me about all of this, but my mother, Aunt Helen and I did our share of gossiping about the double romance situation in the neighboring house.

FIRE ON THE MOUNTAIN

One hot summer day Gramma and I were sitting on the front porch in our rocking chairs and looking up towards the Upper Mountain Road we saw billows of black smoke rising. Then we heard the clang of fire engines. Sadly it was Harry Hill's house and it burned to the ground. Afterwards The Hills moved in next door with the Dickinsons. At some point Harry married Fanny and Glenn married Margie. Fanny became Fanny Hill and Margie became Margie Dickinson. Margie had red hair which was cut short and parted on the side. She was in her 20's and somewhat overweight. On top of that she was very "simple." Gramma said that she was not like Harold, "not quite right", but she was very naive. She relied on my grandmother and my aunts to help her with her finances and child-rearing.

Margie and Glenn eventually had two children of their own, Bobby and Helen. Helen was named after my Aunt Helen whom Margie adored. I was never allowed to play with Bobby or Helen. I wasn't quite sure why but assumed it was because they were much younger. I did used to watch them from the front yard as they stood behind the boxwood bushes that separated the two front yards. Bobby had sandy colored curly hair and Helen had white blond straight hair. When Bobby spoke to me across the bushes I could not understand what he was saying. Helen seemed sharper and more alert. My grandmother and aunts often commented on how Helen and Bobby never seemed to catch the diseases that we did such as measles and chickenpox. The fact that we were always scrubbing and cleaning apparently made no difference to childhood diseases.

Margie would purchase items from Uncle Sam the Grocery Man and then come over to ask Gramma what she had bought. Once she purchased a Pin-up Radio and had no idea what it was for. But Glenn adored her and they seemed to be very much in love. They had a new baby girl one summer who died. I'm not sure what happened, perhaps it was SIDS, sudden infant death syndrome. All I do remember is that Glenn came over to Gramma's with the dead little baby wrapped in a towel. He was taking her on the Greyhound bus to a funeral parlor in Lockport. I remember we all went to the funeral. After that they did not have any other children.

Harry Hill used to come over by himself to visit Gramma and Uncle Eddie. He was a very exuberant man and Uncle Eddie laughed a lot when Harry visited. I remember one time when he was visiting and Uncle Eddie inquired, "Well, Harry, how is everything going for you?"

"Well, Ed, I've got three fine white horses, and Fanny's got the piles."

My Uncle Eddie laughed so hard, we never forgot it and over the year we all adopted Harry's phrase when we're asked how things are going. "I've got three fine white horses and Fanny's got the piles."

SUMMER OF 1944

The July heat was sweltering and strangely, instead of sitting under the Horse Chestnut tree, Grampa had come up on the front porch and started taking off his clothes. Gramma immediately sensed that something was wrong. "Jean, run over to your Aunt Esther's and tell her I need help, that Grampa is having an attack."

Attack? I took off like a rocket down the porch steps and headed down the road to the path through the fields and across the railroad tracks. By the time I ran into their back yard and found Aunt Esther I couldn't talk. My heart was racing, my breath was almost gone and when I opened my mouth, no words came out.

"Jean....Jean....what's wrong? Is it Gramma?" I shook my head no. "Is it Grampa?" I nodded yes. Somehow she called my Uncle Pete and they drove over. When I caught my breath and walked back Grampa was in his big bed in the front room and Dr. Cole was on his way. Grampa seemed to be heavily sleeping, and I found out later he had gone into a coma.

All the family was notified and Aunt Helen was the first to appear. While she and Grampa had a stormy past, she was overwhelmed with sadness. I overheard her crying over his bed, "Poppa...poppa...can you hear me? I love you."

Gramma retreated into stoicism. One by one the family arrived to say goodbye to their father. Aunt Helen investigated the possibility of having Uncle Emmett sent home from Europe but even she could not change the war situation. We sat up for three nights listening to Grampa's snoring and heavy breathing which resounded from his bedroom clear into the living room. Each family member took turns sitting by his bedside. On the third night we all heard an owl in the tree outside the living room and Gramma said, "He's gone." And he was.

FAMILY FROM NEW JERSEY

Uncle Tommy, Aunt Lizzie and my two cousins, Bill and Eddie, arrived from New Jersey for the funeral. Grampa was laid out in his bedroom where the bed had been taken down and replaced by his casket. For three days many people filed in and out of the house expressing their condolences. Aunt Helen made sure everyone in our family had black dresses or suits for the funeral and generally organized everything

.

Grampa had succumbed to hardening of the arteries. I'm not sure what his attack had been but there was no blood to be seen. The attack however had affected his brain and that had caused the coma. I was afraid to spend any time in the casket room because I was sure I could still hear his breathing. Sitting for long periods of time in the living room I noticed a plaque on the wall next to his favorite chair. It noted that in World War I Uncle Billy had taken part in the Battle of Chateau-Thierry. This may have been where he suffered from mustard gas.

Gramma had gone around covering all the mirrors (an old Irish custom) in the house, while Aunt Helen was lifting them up to check how she looked. No radio or music was allowed and we could not play cards which was one of the few pleasures available to us. When I asked about the mirrors I was told it was "a custom". I learned later it had something to do with spirits being unable to see their images.

The day of the funeral several cars were provided by the funeral parlor for all the Degan family. We all crowded together in the living room and the funeral director called out the family names one-by-one in order of birth. First, Gramma was called and Uncle Eddie accompanied her, than the Martin Degan family, followed by all members of the families of Uncle Tommy, Aunt Esther, my mother Dorothy, and Aunt Helen. At this time Aunt Helen and Uncle Al had no children. While it was sad to lose Grampa, the family continued on after the funeral with a typical Irish wake which included much drinking of beer, laughing, singing and of course an occasional argument. Uncle Tommy was particularly shaken by the death. He felt very close to his father despite living so far away, and tended to blame Gramma for the distance between she and Grampa.

I began to better know my two cousins from New Jersey. After the funeral we went to the upstairs bedroom and played cards. Their personalities and their looks were entirely different. Bill was 16 then and taller than Eddie or I who had not yet turned 12. Bill's blond curly hair and brown eyes were a contrast to Eddie's blue eyes and darker brown hair. Eddie talked a mile-a-minute and couldn't seem to sit still while Bill spoke slowly with a quiet air of confidence. I was a mixture of both of them with light brown hair, blue eyes and about the same height as Eddie. We were often mistaken for brother and sister until Eddie would start talking with his New Jersey accent. I was enthralled with Bill's handsome appearance and his kind manner. I knew he had been studying for the priesthood and that even garnered my admiration more.

One day about a week after the funeral Bill and I were taking the bus at Gasport to go to Lockport to stay with Aunt Helen. While we were waiting for the bus in front of Jones' Drugstore a young girl in her teens dropped a whole handful of pennies and they scattered all over the sidewalk. I was snickering with embarrassment for her, but Bill immediately stepped forward and picked up every single penny and handed it to the shy girl. He didn't seem to care what other people thought but instinctively did the right thing. I never forgot that gesture and my admiration for him grew a hundred fold. He was unassuming and didn't seem to be aware of his handsomeness or attractiveness to others--especially women.

JUDY

Maybe it was because Gramma was sad about Uncle Emmett leaving, or it could have just been a coincidence, but Uncle Eddie surprised us by bringing home a puppy. She was a little blond very curly-haired cocker spaniel with large brown eyes and curly floppy ears that almost hung down to the floor. I'm not sure whether Gramma or Uncle Eddie named her "Judy" but she fit the name. It was my first dog. Living in Buffalo could have been the reason why my parents did not get us a dog. Or maybe my dad couldn't abide with another female in the house.

Judy was pampered, babied and overfed. You could hear her toenails clacking over the kitchen linoleum floor or the cement sidewalk until Uncle Eddie would clip them. If Gramma thought I would be coming to Gasport for the weekend she would buy a cake, and if I didn't show up she fed it to Judy. It wasn't long before Judy's stomach was dragging on the floor. But she was spunky and loved to be combed and petted. Gramma and I would spend hours combing burdocks out of her curls, and if that didn't work they were clipped off with a scissors. And there were plenty of burdock bushes in the fields behind the house. Gramma loved having Judy around.

Uncle Eddie announced one day, "Jean, we're going to take Judy hunting. She should be able to raise some pheasants" It wasn't pheasant season but we were just going out to practice and see if Judy would know what to do. Uncle Eddie had a gigantic 12 gauge shotgun and he carried it with him so Judy would get used to it. Off we went into the fields behind the house with Judy running ahead of us through the tall grass. You couldn't even see her, only the grass spreading apart. All of a sudden we heard a rustling noise and a big pheasant flew up into the air. Uncle Eddie was pleased as punch.

"Good dog!" Uncle Eddie said and Judy came running back towards us with his tongue hanging out and looking exhausted. Judy was not in shape. Too much cake I'm afraid.

Judy went upstairs with Gramma and I to go to bed every night and curled up at the end of Gramma's bed. From the other bedroom where I slept I wasn't sure if Gramma or Judy was snoring.

Judy would give you her paw if you asked, and she would sit if you said, "Sit!" Eddie would throw a stick into the yard and Judy would fetch it and bring it back panting as she ran. Other than this Judy's main purpose seemed to be having someone pet and comb her. I talked to her about things and she was a terrific listener. I am sure she knew exactly what I told her, and she definitely told no one--not even Gramma.

BILL AND EDDIE ARE LEFT BEHIND

Aunt Lizzie and Uncle Tommy decided to leave Bill and Ed behind as they returned to New Jersey. The boys had mixed feelings but went along with their parent's decision. Bill went to stay with Aunt Helen in Lockport, since Uncle Al was away in the army. Eddie spent part of the time with me at Gramma's and part of the time at The Gormley's where he could be with his other cousins Ed and Nancy who were two years younger than us. For me it was great to have someone my own age. I would get permission from Gramma to walk through the back fields and go over to The Gormley's to play with Nancy, Eddie Gormley, and Eddie Degan.

Uncle Pete would take us all to Lockport to the movies to see cowboy films and when we came home we would make our own movie version. Nancy insisted on being Dale Evans, Eddie D., wanted to be Roy Rogers and that left Eddie G. to be Gabby Hayes and I made up another female character. We did have some play guns and holsters and used sticks and wooden horses to pretend to ride on. Usually we got along fairly well but there were times when Eddie D. and I would sulk off back to Gramma's till things cooled down. Nancy was very emotional and easily offended.

Eddie D. and I would then get our bathing suits on and trek off through the backyard path to Mirror Lake. I did not know how to swim so I would take an inner tube and admire Eddie as he swam from one side of the shallow end to the other.

"Come on, Jean, you can do it...just stand in the water here...it's only up to your neck. Now, just dunk your head in the water and try to float," Eddie would say. It took many days and much encouragement from Eddie before I was able to float, tread water and finally do the dog paddle. I think it must have been near the end of that summer before I really felt safe enough to abandon the inner tube. We were not paying the 35 cents to get in because of the agreement with Art Shaffer and my Uncle Eddie, but one summer day we were "caught".

A tall teenage worker at the lake came down to the shallow end to check out if we had paid. His name was Ed Smith and I'll never forget his accusing voice. "So...did you two pay the 35 cents to get in?"

"No, we just live in the back here and my Uncle Eddie...."

"I don't care WHERE you live or WHO you are...you are committing a sin by swimming here without paying."

We looked at each other and began to grab our towels and head home. It was obvious we could not argue with this angry man. Then he screamed, "VENGEANCE IS MINE SAYS THE LORD!" as we ran through the back fields.

Eddie and I tried to figure out if vengeance is the lord's, why was ED SMITH treating us with so much vengeance. We told Uncle Eddie when he came home and he said he would talk to Art Shaffer, but I don't think he ever did. Instead we decided to swim in the Erie Barge Canal--which was free but also against the law. After Ed Smith we decided we'd take our chances with the State! We never told Gramma where we were going but would put our bathing suits on under our clothes, take our towels and go uptown to Gasport. There is a lift bridge there crossing the canal and we would jump from the railing and swim to the shore. The tide in the canal is quite strong, so depending on which side of the bridge we would jump from, we either had to swim against the tide or let it take us under the bridge. We also had to be aware of any oncoming barges which we had been warned could "suck us under the boat."

The canal was brown and murky but it was cool, refreshing and free. The man who tended the bridge saw us and other young people jumping into the canal but never bothered us. And when we could manage to get 35 cents we would go to Mirror Lake and stay at the deep end where there was a raft about 30 feet from shore. Eddie and I would try to make each other laugh as we tried to swim out to the raft, so we got in the habit of carrying a small beach ball with us to cling onto when the foolishness started.

One Sunday, Ed's brother Bill came down from Lockport to visit and went to Mirror Lake with us. First he pushed Ed off the raft when he wasn't expecting it and then threatened to do the same to me. But we fixed him. We waited till he was about halfway out to the raft, and Ed and I both started acting so silly that Bill almost drowned trying to reach us. We managed to escape before he reached the raft because we knew what our fate might be if he caught us.

Nancy and Eddie Gormley were not allowed to go to Mirror Lake for fear they might drown, and we felt sad for them on the hot days that we enjoyed Mirror Lake and the canal. They couldn't believe we were actually swimming in the canal which was right across from their house.

TRIPS TO LOCKPORT

Ed and I also would go to Lockport to visit Bill and stay at Aunt Helen's house. One of the benefits of this was that we could go to the baseball game. Aunt Helen lived on the corner of Hawley Street which was only a few blocks to Outwater Park and the baseball field. The admission was 35 cents each and Aunt Helen would give us beer bottles to return for two cents each. And we would save our pennies during the week. Bill, Ed and I would march off to the game with hands full of pennies and Aunt Helen would give us extra money for hot dogs or soda. We felt rich! And Lockport had a fairly good baseball team.

On the main road between Gasport and Lockport a drive-in theater was erected. Of course we didn't have a car or money, but the three of us would hitchhike or walk the three miles to the theater. We had to carry blankets with us because of the mosquitoes, but we would sit under the trees behind all the cars in the back of the theater and enjoy the latest movies. On the way through a field next to the theater we discovered a peach orchard with gigantic lush ripe peaches and would each pick one to enjoy during the movie--again hoping no one would catch us. The drive-in also had public bathrooms and a snack bar which we frequented when we had money. As I recall, Bill had found a part-time job and would give Ed and I money when he had it. The Gormley's weren't allowed to come with us to the driveway, but we would tell them all about the movies when we went there.

A SURPRISE FOR EDDIE AND BILL

Eddie had only brought a few clothes with him for Grampa's funeral and when his mother and father went back to New Jersey they promised to send him clothes for the summer on a Greyhound Bus. Every day Eddie and I would go up to the drugstore for the newspapers, mail and hope that the bus would bring Eddie his clothes. In the meantime, Aunt Esther had given him some clothes of her son Ed. One day a suitcase did arrive and the only thing in it was a pair of knickers. Ed and I knew something was not right! I didn't know any history about his parents, but he told me that he was afraid they might be drinking. Actually, that is exactly what had happened. I'm not sure if
it was the death of Grampa or what, but when they returned to Paterson, they went on a big binge. It ended with both of them losing their jobs and selling all of their possessions and moving to Gasport to live with Gramma. Eddie was devastated. He had many friends in Paterson and, after living in a big city, here he was in the small town of Gasport. He tried to make the best of it but I could tell it was sad for him.

THINGS IMPROVE

It didn't take Uncle Tommy long to find a job as a Janitor at North Park School in

Lockport. He bought a car and stopped drinking. I found out that Uncle Tommy was an alcoholic, which meant he could not just have a beer without going overboard. The only way was for him to not have even one drink. Despite this problem he was a wonderful eccentric guy. A bright man he was also very witty and Aunt Lizzie was the butt of many of his jokes. She didn't seem to mind and they made a great pair.

The good news about Uncle Tommy's job was that he worked nights at the school.
Eddie and I would go to work with him many nights and have the run of the school. We would go to the gym and play basketball or ping pong half the night. Then we would lie on the gym mats and sleep for a few hours until morning when Uncle Tommy would finish
his shift and take us back to Gasport. We were always careful to put everything back and not break anything. Sometimes Uncle Tommy would give us each an ice cream skippy cup which he paid for on the cash register. Somehow we managed to get through the day without falling asleep after being up most of the night.

HIKING UP TO THE MOUNTAIN ROAD

"Jean, let's pack a lunch and hike up to the mountain road," Eddie said one day. Sounded like a neat idea to me. We had sat on the front porch looking up at the mountain (actually a hill) enough but had never explored it.

We packed peanut butter and jelly sandwiches in two small bags and took bottles of water. At that time a new road was being built right across from East Avenue called the Rochester Road. Pavement was being laid as we trekked across it to the foot of the mountain/hill. Even though it was hot, as soon as we got across the field and under the trees, it was definitely much cooler. The evergreen trees were so tall we couldn't believe it and the rocks were enormous. We saw where big mounds of moss was growing on giant rocks. It was steep but we kept going up and up until we reached a spot where we decided to eat our lunches. We sat on a big rock and as soon as we opened our bags, thousands of mosquitoes descended on us.

"I can't eat anything, my sandwich is covered with mosquitoes," Ed yelled.
I kept swatting the mosquitoes off my arms and trying to cover up. Throwing the bags away, we climbed up to the top of the mountain and finally were standing on Upper Mountain Road. From there we looked down through the trees and Gramma's house looked like a tiny toy house.

"Let's just walk to the end of this road where there is another road that will take us back to East Avenue," Eddie said. I agreed. I didn't want to go through the "mosquito village" ever again. Uncle Eddie thought it was hilarious when we told him what had happened to us on our big adventure.

ANOTHER BIG ADVENTURE

Bill had bought himself a B. B. gun and, believe it or not, we had to go to Buffalo to purchase B. B.s for it. Bill said we could hitchhike.

"The three of us?" I said.

"Sure. We'll take Judy, too." Bill replied.

"I don't want to go if Judy is going. She'll run into the road," Eddie added.

For once Eddie was right. We decided to leave Judy at home -- no doubt to eat cake.

Downtown Buffalo was about 25 miles away and we had never hitchhiked so far. Gramma had no idea where we were off to. We told her we were "going shopping" for things for Bill's B. B. gun.

We crossed East Avenue and went onto the "new road" or Rochester Road and started walking towards the drive-in movie theater. The first problem was that I was too shy to put out my thumb but sort of hung back behind Eddie and Bill as they walked backwards so drivers could see their faces. Bill was even carrying his B. B. gun. Why anyone in their right mind would pick up three young kids with a gun is beyond me, but some man stopped and we all piled into the car.

"Where ya' headed?" he said as he looked in the rear view mirror at Eddie and I. Bill sat in the front seat next to the driver.

"We're going to Buffalo to buy some B. B.'s for my new gun" replied Bill.

"You two in the back seat sister and brother?" the man asked

"Yeah," Ed said. It was easier than going into explanations about cousins, etc.

He took us as far as Swormsville which is about half way. We tumbled out of the car there and had no idea which way to go towards Buffalo. Someone had tried to paint over the "Swormsville" sign and remove the "S" so it looked like "Wormsville" and we had big laughs about anyone having to live in Wormsville. Almost as bad as GASport.

Finally we figured out that Swormsville was just north of Millersport and we did know where that was, so we started hitchhiking again. I still slunked down next to the boys so no one could see me.

"Jean, why aren't you helping?" Eddie said.

"Cause I don't want anyone to know I want a ride." I replied.

"Oh, God, I can't believe it. WE DO want a ride, don't you?" Bill said.

It was hard to explain. I DID want a ride but I didn't want it to look like I was begging for a ride. If a car stopped and asked I would accept. Judy would have understood.

We walked about a mile before another car picked us up and I thought we would die of thirst. This car took us right into downtown and Bill seemed to know where the B. B. store was located. Bill had money and treated us to some Coca Cola after we bought the B. B.'s. Then we started the trek back again.

"Jean, if you don't put your thumb out, you can't get into a car if it stops!" Eddie warned. So I meekly put out my thumb and a car did stop. After about 4 hours we had managed to make the entire trip to Buffalo and back to Gasport. That was the furthest we ever hitchhiked, and we never told Gramma or my parents.

PICKING CHERRIES

Eddie and I rarely had any money and since we were only 12 years old the chances of getting a job were slim. I did baby sit next door for the three children of Bob and Helen (Genet) Schultz and made a few dollars which I shared with Eddie. We were aware that Mr. Dickinson's sour cherry trees were ready to be harvested and that he was looking for pickers.

"Gramma, do you think Mr. Dickinson would hire Eddie and I to pick his cherries?" I inquired.

"Well, Jean, I don't know. But I will ask him," she replied.

Next day it was all settled. Mr. Dickinson came over to get us and show us his ladders that were set up against the trees along with piles of white boxes for the cherries. All we had to do was climb up the ladders and fill our boxes. Mr. Dickinson would then weigh the boxes and we would be paid 2 cents a pound.

Eddie wasn't afraid to climb up to the very top of the trees but I kept to the lower branches. Although the late July day was hot, when I was up on the ladder inside the tree leaves and branches it was cool. But there were the ever-present bees buzzing in and out and the flies alighting on the sticky limbs. Mr. Dickinson had other adult pickers who seemed quite adept at swiftly filling their boxes.

"I don't think I could ever do this for a living, Eddie." He nodded in agreement.

Once you got all the cherries within reach you had to move the ladder and make sure it was laying against a sturdy limb. The cherries weren't really good for eating because they were so sour, but were good for pies or jams. Finally, it was noon and we broke for lunch and went back to Gramma's kitchen where she had peanut butter and jelly sandwiches for us. Our hands and arms were all red and sticky and I had pieces of tree leaves and branches sticking in my braids. Gramma looked at us with pity in her eyes, and after lunch we headed back and up the trees again.

At the end of the day when all the boxes were weighed we each made about $2.50. We felt like millionaires and were planning on how the next day we were going to double our pickings. After about three days the cherry trees were bare and we were exhausted. And we were six or seven dollars richer. Mr. Dickinson loaded up all the cherries in his Model T Ford and drove off to the market to sell them. Gramma was proud of our tenacity and told everyone what good workers we were.

NOT REALLY OUR COUSIN

Three houses up East Avenue from Gramma's house and over the bridge Uncle Al's sister Lorraine, her husband and two children lived. Her one son named Patrick was the same age as Eddie and I, and upstairs inside his barn was a basketball "court". The room was the entire length of the barn and had a basketball hoop at one end. Aunt Helen told us that Patrick and his brother Jamie were our "cousins by marriage" but Eddie and I didn't believe he was related to us at all. I sort of had a crush on Patrick and I didn't want to believe he was my real cousin in case marriage might be in our future.

In the cold weather we spent endless hours inside the barn shooting baskets and thinking up things to do to pass the time. I can't remember that we ever had homework or any kind of schoolwork to do. School work was confined to what we did IN school.

Patrick decided one day that it would be fun if we played a joke on Aunt Helen. It sounded pretty funny at the time and while I was afraid to cross Aunt Helen I thought that it wasn't really my idea. In any event I was only an observer. I'm not sure why Patrick wanted to embarrass Aunt Helen, but the plot was laid out.

Our next door neighbor, Margie Dickinson adored Aunt Helen. Aunt Helen was kind to her and Margie would have done anything that Aunt Helen asked of her. Pat knew that Aunt Helen was at The Hammond Hotel on a particular Saturday evening with her friends. So he and Eddie wrote a note and gave it to Margie. The note said: "Margie, I have some baby clothes to give you. I am at The Hammond Hotel. Come up here and ask for me and I will give you the clothes."

Well, Margie couldn't read, but she asked her oldest son to read the note to her. Patrick and Eddie were hiding up in the horse chestnut tree watching. Margie, got out her baby buggy and put her little children in it and headed up East Avenue towards The Hammond Hotel. She wore no stockings and run-down sandals and her hair was in a simple straight cut bob. Her dress was spotted with food stains and she looked the worse for wear. I felt a twinge of pity for poor Margie, but Patrick and Eddie went on giggling up in the tree.

When she arrived at The Hammond Hotel she quickly found Aunt Helen. She showed her the note. Aunt Helen was very kind to Margie and told her that she would in fact find some baby clothes for her the next day. Then Aunt Helen came charging home to Gramma's. Patrick and Eddie scattered and although I hid upstairs Aunt Helen cornered me and I spilled the beans. Then she went up to Patrick's house and told his parents what had occurred. They were mortified. Patrick was severely reprimanded as was Eddie. Aunt Helen said I should have tried to stop them but realized that I could not have done it. Gramma was very upset also. I believe that was the last time Patrick tried to play a joke on Aunt Helen. The only good thing to come of it was that Aunt Helen did go and buy some baby clothes for Margie and also gave her some dresses for herself.

THE HORSE CHESTNUT TREE

While the tall large-leafed tree in the front yard afforded a safe place at times for us to hide from the adults, it also provided a cool place in summer under its branches. Grampa would sit on the bench under the tree, and my uncles would spread a blanket over the soft grass where we would lie and stare up into the thick branches. Occasionally a motorist would stop and ask to take a photo of the tree--especially in the Spring when it was in full blossom with its pyramid shaped white and yellow flowers.

I loved that tree as if it were a person. I would put my arms half way around its trunk and feel its warmth and could almost hear the juices bubbling up through it to the leaves and branches. Cousin Ed and I used it as a Jungle Gym. One summer day as we were practicing our exploits, Ed put a step ladder in front of the biggest strong branch. We would leap from the bottom rung of the ladder to grab onto the big limb and swing. Then Ed kept moving the ladder further and further away from the branch to see how far we could leap. On a final leap I missed the branch and fell flat on my back. I didn't know what happened but I felt like I died. Ed took my hand and led me into the house. Gramma was terror stricken. I was not, could not, breathe.

What had happened is that I had the wind knocked out of me. Quite an experience. Somehow I started breathing again, but I had injured the muscles in my back and years later that weakness showed up. It definitely put an end to leaping from the ladder onto the branch. But we still climbed up into the tree for solace, escape and the fantastic view. We climbed as high up as we possibly could. On one occasion we decided to put our initials on the tree: E.D. and J.K. I wonder if they're still there. The tree is at least 20 feet higher now and it was about 30 feet high then.

SUMMER OF '44 ENDS

It had been a great summer of adventures with my newly-discovered cousins from New Jersey and I hated to see it coming to an end. Eddie had been enrolled in school in Gasport and Bill was staying with Aunt Helen and attending Lockport Senior High. I had to return to Buffalo where I would be starting 8th grade at Public School #26. The war rationing was still going on and the butcher shop where my father worked was having trouble getting enough meat for its customers. My father had taken a job at Curtiss-Wright Airplane Factory and was also tending bar at the tavern right on the corner in front of our house.

He worked the evening shift at Curtiss-Wright and put rivets in the planes. He would accidentally bring home many rivets in his work pant's pockets, and I would spend endless amounts of time lining them up as if they were soldiers marching into battle. I had my own little army of rivets to play with. My mother was worried that my two younger sisters would get hold of them and choke to death so I had to be very careful.

I had many friends in our neighborhood in Buffalo and one best friend "Rainy" Claire. Rainy showed me how to shop with the ration coupons and, since my mother was busy with Joanne and Mary Ann, I was the official family shopper. Around the corner from where we lived on Keppel Street was Seneca Street. The Seifert Family lived in a big house on Seneca Street and had five children; Gerald, Earl, Lillian, Myrtle and Joanie and they were all my friends. But, despite all this I missed being in Gasport with my grandmother and cousins. I really had the best of two worlds--the city and the country.

As the summer slipped away, our letters back and forth to Uncle Emmett increased. They had to be written on a sort of tissue paper that was an envelope and letter all in one. It was called V-mail, and there wasn't too much you could put in one of those letters. You just had to write another one. Newspapers were full of accounts of battles in Europe and the islands of the South Pacific and Gramma scanned the latest names of men killed in action. Emmett was still alive.

When I left to go back to school in September I promised Gramma I would be back every weekend that I could manage. Aunt Lizzie came to be a great help to Gramma as she seemed to be suffering the worry about Uncle Emmett and the loss of Grampa. I didn't think she would miss him since they rarely talked, but one day when we were sitting on the front porch in our rocking chairs she looked out at the bench under the tree and said to me, "You know, I miss seeing your grandfather sitting there on the bench under the horse chestnut tree." She rarely expressed her emotions and I did not know how to respond, but I knew she was feeling more sadness than just about Uncle Emmett and Grampa. Perhaps it was the culmination of all of her losses through the years.

THANKSGIVING AND KILLING THE PIG

My parents, sisters and I all piled into our old two-door Chevy car and headed off to Gasport for Thanksgiving with Gramma, Uncle Tommy, Aunt Lizzie, Bill, Eddie and Aunt Helen. When we got there Gramma told us that Mr. Dickinson was going to slaughter his pig in the afternoon. He had the big sow in the field directly across from our house. There was about two or three inches of clean white snow on the ground but the temperature was not that cold. Neither Ed nor I had ever seen an animal slaughtered before and thought it would be quite exciting. Joanne and Mary Ann were told to stay in the house. We put on our winter jackets, boots and gloves and crossed the road to where the large pig was standing in the middle of the field. We leaned against the 4 foot high fence surrounding the pen and watched as Mr. Dickinson entered. He had his typical cap pulled down low on his ears and was carrying a long metal rod in one hand. We had no idea what he was going to do with the long rod, thinking instead that he was going to shoot the pig.

We watched intently as he circled the pig who seemed to sense that something wasn't quite right. Mr. Dickinson came closer and closer to the big sow with the long rod in his hand. Suddenly he lifted up the rod and shoved it straight between the pig's eyes and into its forehead. Eddie and I were speechless as the pig's red blood squirted all over the white snow. The pig flopped over to one side and died instantly. The rod had gone straight through its brain. I felt sick to my stomach and wanted to go right home but Ed said, "Don't be a baby, let's see what's going to happen now." I wished I had gone home. Mr. Dickinson took a large knife and sliced the pig open from end to end in one swoop. Then he grabbed each side and hung them from the tree in the corner of the yard. There the pig hung dripping blood red blood all over the white snow as Mr. Dickinson proudly point out to us the insides.

"Now, look here, that's where the bacon comes from, and here's the ham and pork chops..." I swore to myself never to eat those foods again. Thankfully, Gramma called over to us that Thanksgiving dinner was ready. We came back to the house but I could hardly eat anything. All I could see was that rod being stabbed into the pig's forehead and then all of its insides exposed as it hung from the tree.

GERMANY SURRENDERS - MAY 1945

The combined forces of the United States, Britain, Free French and allied troops in Germany finally resulted in the surrender of Germany on May 7, 1945. Uncle Emmett had survived the war. His letters spoke about how his Reconnaissance forces were now hunting German S. S. soldiers who were attempting to hide out in the countryside. In one letter he wrote, "My buddies and I went out today and shot a peasant, and then ate it." I was horrified. Gramma said, "I think he misspelled "pheasant". That was a relief. I just pictured he and his buddies killing a peasant and eating him. While Uncle Emmett was rounding up S.S. soldiers the rest of the free world was celebrating the end of the war in Europe. Discoveries were made of concentration camps where millions of Jews had been slaughtered. Everyone one shocked with the photos in the newspapers of these atrocities. We knew Uncle Emmett would have many stories to tell us when he returned. But, somehow, Gramma was still uneasy about him being so far away even though the war there was over. The war with Japan was still going on and we were losing many soldiers in the battles for South Pacific Islands. Uncle Al was still somewhere in the Pacific but Aunt Helen was sure he was in a safe place.

EIGHTH GRADE GRADUATION - JUNE 1945

In October of 1944 I had turned 12 years old, and Richard Schwartz and I, who had both skipped third grade were the youngest eighth graders. As was the custom there would be a regular graduation ceremony in the auditorium of Public School #26. I had been asked to be part of the program by reading a letter from the superintendent. To this day I can recite the first two lines, "1945 will go down in history as..." well, maybe the first few *words*. I memorized it for weeks. My little sister Joanne, who was in First Grade
at Public School #26 was also asked to be part of the program. She was a very pretty and well-spoken girl of seven years old. Her long dirty-blond curly hair added much to her appearance along with those big blue "Degan" eyes. I was very proud that she had been chosen from the whole school as the only presenter that was not an eighth grader.

All my relatives had been invited to the ceremony, but Gramma was unable to make the trip to Buffalo. I never knew her to ride in a car or a bus, and I used to tell her that as soon as I was 16 years old I would get a license and come and take her for a ride. She only smiled at this promise, but in retrospect I was probably the last person she would entrust to her safety--a 16-year-old driver.

Graduation day, June 22, 1945, finally arrived and as I stepped onto the stage with my Superintendent's Letter in hand, I glanced out and saw my Aunt Helen, my Uncle Joe and Aunt Helen (father's brother), my parents and my little sister Mary Ann just being seated. I panicked! Even though I knew the letter by heart, I put the paper up in front of my face and began to READ it! The paper was shaking from my hands and I read the letter so fast, I don't think anyone knew what it said--only me who knew it by-heart! Then Joanne strode out onto the stage and presented her speech as cool as a cucumber. Everyone clapped. No stage fright for her.

Afterwards we all went back to my house and the beer flowed freely. We took pictures and I received a beautiful card from my grandmother with money in it. Aunt Helen gave me her beautiful blue camera with the pull-out lens and my interest in photography started. The school year was over and I was ready to head back to Gasport, Gramma, my cousins and summer vacation!

SUMMER OF 1945

The summer turned out to be exquisite. Now that I had learned to swim and hitchhike, Ed, Bill and I had further adventures. Eddie and I managed to buy some used tennis rackets and taught ourselves how to play at the tennis courts at the old Gasport High School. We both had used bicycles--one had a pedal on one side with only a bar where the rubber part had fallen off. You had to be really careful as your foot kept slipping off, but the bikes gave us new freedom and greatly enlarged our world.

Uncle Pete and Aunt Esther had sold the house in Gasport that Grampa built and bought a farm in Barker. Uncle Pete had purchased two work horses, "Nell" and "Belle", who he hitched up to a plow and planted corn, wheat, tomatoes and potatoes. They had chickens, and bantam roosters in a coop and got fresh milk from a neighbor. The farm house was a large two story white frame with a wrap-around veranda and a large barn next to the chicken coop some distance from the house. The barn was full of hay and Ed, Nancy and her brother Eddie, and myself would climb up on the beams and catapult ourselves down into the dusty hay. Nancy and Eddie could do somersaults off the beams but all I could bring myself to do was jump straight down. No catapulting for me.

When it was time to take the horses for water, Uncle Pete would let us take turns riding on Nell and Bell. The horses must have been 12 or 15 years old, and I don't believe I ever saw them do anything close to a gallop. They just meandered along to the well for water and pulled the plow with Uncle Pete behind. Uncle Pete sometimes displayed a temper when the horses weren't cooperating and would start punching them in the sides as if he was still in the boxing ring. Nancy would shriek with terror when she saw this happening and was sure Nell and Bell would be killed.

The house in Barker was about 12 miles from Gramma's in Gasport and one hot summer day Ed and I decided to ride our bikes to the farm. Ed took the bike with the broken pedal and we took a bottle with some water. It was the longest 12 miles I ever remember and seemed to take forever to arrive. We stopped once under some shade trees in Hartland to cool off and catch our breath. When we finally rode into the driveway Aunt Esther couldn't believe her eyes that we had come all that way on our bikes. She fixed us a great dinner of roast chicken, fresh corn, tomatoes, hot biscuits and homemade chocolate and lemon meringue pies. No wonder we loved going there.

After dinner, Uncle Pete got out his guitar and sang cowboy songs. Margaret and Mary, the twins, who were in their teens put on a variety show for us and Aunt Esther popped corn for us to eat while we enjoyed the fun. We stayed overnight and after a big country breakfast we headed back to Gasport. This meant pedaling uphill the last few miles from Hartland to Gasport.

Bill was still living in Lockport with Aunt Helen where he had found a summer job so Ed and I were on our own. We were going into work at night with Ed's father, Uncle Tommy, to North Park School in Lockport, and playing basketball all evening. Daytimes we were swimming either in the Erie Canal or Mirror Lake and playing tennis at the high school. I was still writing daily letters for Gramma to Uncle Emmett and going to the post office for his replies. Ed and I would go and pick up the newspapers on our bikes now and have our sundaes and Coca Colas together. He was still missing his friends in New Jersey and probably wished I were a boy, but he didn't complain and managed to invent things for us to do every day.

One day he decided we should go fishing in Mirror Lake and bring home some fresh fish for Gramma. We didn't realize that the only fish there were carp--and not very suitable for eating being referred to as the "garbage-eating fish". Despite this we made fishing poles out of tree branches and tied string on them and dug up worms for bait. We only had to buy fish hooks. I thought it would be fun, but when we got to the lake I couldn't/wouldn't squish the worm onto the hook so Ed had to do it for me. I actually caught a carp and pulled it up onto the ground where it commenced to flip and flop all over because I would not take it off the hook. Just thinking about the hook and how it would tear the fish's mouth to take it out made me weak. Ed took it off the hook and put it on a stick that I had to carry home.

"No, Jean, no one is going to CARRY your fish for you. I did everything else. YOU carry it," Ed said. Halfway home through the path towards the back of Gramma's house the fish started flipping up and down on the stick and blood was running down it's side. I dropped the stick and ran all the way home. Ed said he would never take me fishing again--and I was glad.

AUGUST 6, 1945

On this date we all learned two new words, "Atomic Bomb." The headlines in the newspapers I picked up at Joneses' drug store were in giant ten-inch letters. The United States had dropped an atomic bomb on Hiroshima, Japan. Everyone in the family had varied opinions about it, from "It's payback for Pearl Harbor" to "It is terrible killing all those innocent civilians." President Harry S Truman had made the decision in an effort to stop the killing and the war. Japan kept fighting. On August 9th a second atomic bomb was dropped on Nagasaki, and on August 14th Japan surrendered. World War II was totally over and Uncle Al would be coming home from the Asian front.

Gramma carefully read every newspaper account in both the Buffalo Evening News and The Lockport Sun & Journal, and she and Mr. Dickinson discussed all the ramifications of the war's end and the atomic bomb. Harry Truman was vilified by some and praised by others. There was no color television then to see the terrible devastation in Hiroshima and Nagasaki but we imagined it. And when I went to the movies, the black and white newsreels showed the horror. The war had resulted in a prospering United States economy but now the war-time jobs were coming to an end. My father's job at Curtiss-Wright airplane factory ended and he spent more time tending bar. There were still shortages of meat, butter and sugar, but that would soon be over as thousands of soldiers would be returning home. Many would take advantage of the G.I. Bill and go on to college because jobs were scarce.

My concerns then were more selfish. In September I would be attending my first year of high school at South Park Annex on Bailey Avenue in Buffalo. It was a little frightening going to a new school with students from other South Buffalo schools. I had attended Public School Number 26 for all of my eight school years. Many of my former classmates were headed to parochial high schools and only Mildred Drazak from my street would be attending South Park. We planned on walking to school together about a two mile walk down Bailey Avenue and over the railroad trestle. I knew it would be a cold walk during the famous Buffalo winters and wished I could stay right in Gasport with Gramma, Uncle Eddie, Uncle Tommy, Aunt Lizzie and cousin Ed.

THE DREAM

I woke up all sweaty with mixed feelings of joy and dread. It was a dream so clear, so vivid that I felt as if it had really happened. Uncle Emmett was standing in a grassy field on crutches with some type of metal rod at the bottom of his one foot. He was dressed in full army-brown uniform, cap and all, and he was smiling his wide grin. Emmett hadn't sent us photos since he was in Europe but I was sure I had been with him IN PERSON. I leaped out of bed and ran downstairs to the kitchen where Gramma was just hoisting a fresh pail of well water up onto the side of the sink.

"Gramma...Gramma...I had a dream with Uncle Emmett." She sat right down in her rocker and looked at me intently.

"Tell me exactly what you saw in the dream." And I did--every detail. "Did Emmett say anything?"

"No, he just smiled," I assured her, keeping one part of the dream to myself.

Gramma looked worried. She did not like the idea of something being wrong with his foot. I had never seen anyone with metal under their foot even though I knew what a cast on a broken arm or leg looked like. That afternoon I had a strange eerie feeling when I went to the post office and saw the red and blue airmail envelope in our box. Even when I touched the letter it felt strange in my hands. I knew instinctively that there was something very important in it.

Gramma was waiting on the front porch in her rocking chair and I held the letter up as soon as I was in her eyesight. She opened it immediately and began to read: "Hi, Ma, I'm writring from the hospital on base. I accidentally dropped a box of ammunition on my foot when we were unloading a truck. I'm on crutches and have a cast on my right foot. I'll be out of commission for awhile and be able to rest."

I was stunned. Just like in my dream. Gramma was not at all surprised. She also "knew" things. Despite Emmett's assurances, I still felt uneasy. The thing I *didn't* tell Gramma about the dream was that Emmett had said, "Goodbye" to me and to tell Gramma. I put that knowledge in the back of my mind. It was too scary to deal with. But I never forgot the dream and began to be afraid of this ability to dream things before they happened/or at least before we officially knew about them.

It didn't make any sense that Emmett had said "goodbye" because the war in Europe and Asia was over and he only had a broken foot. He was smiling. He was fine. But...he said, "goodbye", and he appeared so real that I felt I could have touched him. I told no one else then about the dream except Gramma. We would continue to write to him and soon he would be home and I would be a freshman in high school.

AFTER THE DREAM

"We regret to inform you that Technician 5th Grade Emmett J. Degan died in the service of his country in the European area on October 8, 1945." The telegram was addressed to Gramma, Mary Ann Degan, but it was delivered to the Postmaster in Gasport, John L. Mack.

John L. Mack knew everyone in town personally and knowing that the news would shock and destroy Gramma, he held the wire and contacted Uncle Tommy and Uncle Eddie who decided to keep the news from her as long as possible.

Uncle Emmett had contracted pneumonia while he was recuperating on the base. After a few months of no letters from Uncle Emmett, Gramma surmised the worst. She went into a deep depression and took to her bed. She had moved her bedroom downstairs where Grampa used to sleep and Aunt Lizzie waited on her and tried to get her to eat. Her heart was getting weaker all the time.

ANOTHER TELEGRAM

I was growing more concerned about Gramma's health every day and it was no surprise when we received a telegram from Aunt Helen saying, "Ma is getting worse. Come soon."

I begged my mother to let me take a bus to Gasport and be with Gramma, but she insisted I could not go. Knowing that the situation was dire and not wanting me to witness death first-hand, she would not budge. In the meantime, the whole family prepared to leave for Gasport as soon as my father returned from work. By the time we arrived, Gramma had passed away. The emptiness inside of me felt like as if there were a giant hole in my stomach. And I seemed to be devoid of feelings. There was a numbness that settled in and I could find no tears, no sadness, no anger--nothing but nothingness.

My cousins all came to the house and Ed, Bill and I went upstairs to be alone. We didn't know what to do, so we began playing cards. Aunt Helen came up and began admonishing us for playing cards when Gramma was downstairs in her coffin. I couldn't even relate to that. I felt no shame at playing cards because I still felt nothing. Gramma's body was laid out in the same downstairs bedroom where Grampa had been slightly more than a year before. All the relatives were roaming about the house finding solace in furtive beer drinking and smoking outside. Gramma never permitted smoking in the house and in deference to her, they were not about to change now.

I had come to one large realization. I was no longer afraid of dying, because wherever Gramma was is where I eventually wanted to be. I knew she would welcome me again to be with her. I certainly didn't want to die yet, but having been witness to so many deaths in the family, its inevitability was no secret.

AUNT LIZZIE

(And Family Sayings)

I really got to know Aunt Lizzie after Uncle Tommy and her moved into the house. She was full of witticisms! And when she spieled them off with her New Jersey accent you couldn't help but laugh. Uncle Tommy was definitely *Macho Man* and Aunt Lizzie obeyed his orders. That didn't stop her from commenting on them.

When we were bored and asked to go somewhere or do something, Aunt Lizzie would say, "Sit on the floor and let your legs hang down." By the time we tried to envision this we would be laughing and forget our boredom. If I was upset about not having a boyfriend, Aunt Lizzie would say, "Boys are like streetcars...there'll be another one along any minute." It helped. And if we tried to interrupt the adult conversations, she would firmly remark, "No remarks from the 5 cent's seats". If she saw some young woman swinging her hips walking down the street, she would say, "It must be jelly 'cause jam don't shake like that." Or, on the subject of women, "She can't *cook* but you oughta' see her *can.*"

If we tried to fake illness and not go to school, Aunt Lizzie would catch us right

away. "What's the matter...do you have the *Fli
kerine?*" And when we were really sick, she would announce that we were "Sick-a-bed
on two chairs." If we made a dumb remark, her quick retort was, "You sound like a man
overboard cryin' for more water."
Aunt Lizzie did get upset with Uncle Tommy's bullying and she would walk out the door
saying, "I'm leavin' and there'll be no forwarding address." If we asked her where she
was going she would say, "I'm goin' to *Jibib!*" *Jibib* was nowhere to be found!

I'm not sure if all of these sayings came from New Jersey or just Aunt Lizzie's
family who lived there, but they kept us on our toes. My mother had her own list of
sayings and between her and Aunt Lizzie I had a bagful of quotes to last me a lifetime.
My mother's favorite to me was, "If you don't listen...you must feel." And how right
she was as I muddled through situations the hard way, not listening to her advice.

Some of my favorites: "If you're going to be a thief, don't steal pennies...do it
big." "You can catch a liar quicker than a thief." "A liar has to have the best memory."
"Blood money will do you no good." "He's a house angel and a street devil." And
during the occasional beer parties, "Don't give me shoe-zies when it's boozies that I
want." "Soap is cheap...no one needs to be dirty." "A leopard doesn't change his spots."
"The more you stir it, the worse it stinks." "The least said is the easiest mended." "When
your number's up, your number's up." And I know she stole this one from Wimpy in the
comic strip: "I'll gladly pay you Tuesday for a hamburger today." She especially used
this one on me when I would be nagging for something that I could not afford.

My grandmother's sayings were kinder. When I told her that my cousins were
making fun of my large Kolb ears, she said, "Big ears are a sign of generosity, and I
know that you are generous." It made me feel much better--at least until I could stop
wearing braids and comb my hair over them. In those awkward pre-teen years, I was
kept going by another quote she told me. "That which is beautiful is good, and that
which is good soon too becomes beautiful." I vowed to be very good so that one day
I would become beautiful. I learned that the beauty Gramma was talking about was not
necessarily the physical kind.

COUSIN BILL SURPRISES US!

Bill had been staying with Aunt Helen in Lockport where he had a job and
attended high school, but he did come down and visit us. Uncle Tommy let him drive
his car and we were green with envy. But his big news really took us by surprise.
He had joined the U. S. Marines! My Uncle Tommy and Aunt Lizzie were so proud
they could have burst. Eddie and I were also proud of him. He would be leaving soon
and we were going to drive him to the train in Rochester.

It was a bitter cold Saturday morning in November and a window in Uncle
Tommy's car had broken and there was no time to get it fixed. The snow was coming

down and the roads were slippery, but Bill had to be in Rochester for the 8:00 o'clock train to New York City. Bill drove with Uncle Tommy in the front seat. The back side window was the one that was broken and Aunt Lizzie, Eddie and I huddled in the back seat with our mittens, stocking caps and scarves. As we headed down the road, the snow was flying in the window and we tried to put a piece of cardboard up to deflect it.

By the time we got to the Rochester train station we were like frozen mummies. Uncle Tommy burst into the restaurant in the train station and in his usual gregarious way said to the waitress, "We just blew in from Alaska...and we need some hot coffee. And how about your phone number, too?" Aunt Lizzie just rolled her eyes, and the waitress answered without missing a beat, "You want my grandmother's phone number?" That stopped him cold. We had our coffee and began to thaw out. It wasn't long before the train came and we hugged Bill goodbye.

The next time we saw him was after boot camp when he came home. He looked absolutely fantastic in his uniform with the dark blue jacket and white pants. Eddie and I were sure we would also follow in his footsteps and join the Marines--just for the uniform alone. Uncle Tommy and Aunt Lizzie drove him all over to every member of the family to show him off. When it was time for him to go back to Norfolk, Virginia, we got into Uncle Tommy's car again and went with him all the way.

MOVING TO GASPORT

After the funeral it was decided that my family would move from Buffalo to Gasport. The war had ended and jobs were scarce. My father had lost his job at Curtiss-Wright airplane factory and the meat market had closed. His only job was bartending at the tavern on the corner in front of our house. The summer months gave us time to pack and move to the family homestead. It was where I dreamed of living since I was old enough to understand I had more than one home. In fact besides living in Buffalo, I spent vacations and summers with my aunt and uncle in Lockport and with my grandparents and uncles in Gasport. Of course I loved the summers and vacation times and looked upon Buffalo as school time with cold winters and sharing my parents with my two younger sisters.

The thing is that moving to Gasport was not the panacea I had imagined. First and foremost, Gramma was not there. Secondly the winters were just as cold and school was the same as it was in Buffalo--peer pressure and studying. There was one positive thing--I had "inherited" two "brothers", because my Uncle Tommy, Aunt Lizzie and their two sons, Bill and Eddie had also moved there a year earlier. I had always wished for brothers, or sisters, my own age, and now here they were. Bill and Ed had also moved from a city environment, Paterson, New Jersey as I had from Buffalo. But the others in our rural school, Royalton-Hartland, had been friends and neighbors for many years, so it took time to make friends and be accepted.

I entered into my sophomore year at Royalton-Hartland, and even though Ed and I were almost the same age, I had skipped a grade so he was a freshman. We did manage to make some friends at school, many of whom lived in Middleport. It was necessary to walk about a half mile to get the school bus on Myrtle Avenue and the cold winds blew down East Avenue as we huddled on the corner each morning. There were several times when we skipped school and waited under the bridge on East Avenue until the bus passed. Then we came back and said we had missed the bus. There was much more fun to be had ice skating on the pond or tromping through the woods looking for deer or pheasant.

Every Wednesday afternoon in school we were excused to attend Religious Education. Father Donnelley came to Royalton Hartland school and managed to enroll enough Catholic students to use one classroom. These classes were tiresome, but sometimes funny. He was on a mission to ensure that every student be able to recite the main prayers without error. Every one of us had to stand up, week-after-week and recite "The Our Father", "The Hail Mary", "The Act of Contrition" and "The Nicene Creed." There were about 25 of us in the class which meant you had to listen to each of these prayers at least 25 times. And, if one word was incorrect, you had to start at the beginning and recite the entire prayer again. This went on for the entire year, and Father Donnelley became more irascible as the weeks and months passed by. One thing for sure, we all learned our prayers exactly, because his wrath could reduce the toughest boy to tears. Even now, since many of our prayers have been changed and reworded, I still fear Father Donnelley is going to return and castigate me for not sticking to the original.

I successfully completed my sophomore year and began my junior year at Royalton Hartland. Attending basketball games became a highlight of our lives and Ed and I would take the school bus to Middleport to see them. Our heroes and models were the basketball stars. I joined the girl's basketball team also, and while we played other schools we were seen far less than the boy's basketball team. I also joined the badminton team and was very good at that. All the months that my cousins and I had played basketball, tennis and even football in the back yard paid off in my athletic ability. Unfortunately I was still short compared to the rest of my classmates, and even when I became a senior I was the second shortest in the class at 5 foot 4 inches. So, my athletic career did not go very far.

Because algebra was so difficult for me, I enrolled in a business course and learned shorthand and typing. While it was not considered a college-entrance course, these skills became invaluable for me when it was time to find a job. My father had been right when he advised me to "learn a trade...no one can ever take that away from you." At the time I thought he was only saying that because he had been taught a trade by his father--to be a butcher--and was always able to find employment with that skill. But I sure didn't want to be a butcher. The trade I learned was business and it has been invaluable for me.

(Bill Degan - In the Marines - 1948)

(D. Jean Kolb)

(Top: Twins Mary & Margaret Gormley
Bottom: Nancy & Ed Gormley)

(Esther (Degan) Gormley)

(Ed Gormley, D. Jean Kolb,
Nancy Gormley)

THE AFTERMATH

After Gramma died, Uncle Eddie began drinking on a steady basis. His boss at the lumberyard called him in one morning.

"Ed, you've worked at Standish-Jones for many years driving our lumber trucks all over Western New York. The thing is we've been told that you're drinking while on the road. We're concerned about you--and others. When your truck has a full load of lumber, it's a danger to you and everyone else."

"So, are you firing me?", Uncle Eddie politely asked.

"No...no...Ed. We want to offer you a job right here in the office. You know everything about the business, but we want you off the road."

I could have predicted the Degan response.

"Thanks for the offer, but if I can't be on the road, I quit." And Uncle Eddie walked out of the lumberyard office for the final time of his life. This gave him more time to stay at home and drink. Uncle Eddie was not a mean drunk. The more he drank the wittier he became--and the sicker. We watched his health deteriorate, and his wit increase. He lost not only his mother, but his career which had given him the freedom of the road along with stops at the various bars on his route.

Previously, a meticulous dresser, he now wore the same outfit every day. We could hear the sound of his big brown wing-tipped dress shoes every morning as he came downstairs from his bedroom. He would appear in the living room doorway wearing a red and black checkered wool shirt and baggy levis all frayed around the cuffs hanging over the brown wing tips.

"Good morning little monsters", he would say to all of us kids. "What have you cooked up today?"

We just watched as he headed outside to the outdoor toilet where we knew he had stashed a bottle of beer the night before. When he returned, my mother would try to encourage him to eat something. "I'll just have some coffee, Dot." His hands would be shaking and his skin color ashen. He particularly liked to taunt my younger sister, Joanne, very vocal for her age.

"So, how is 'mouth almighty' this morning?" he would say.

Despite Joanne only being 7 years old she would respond in kind. "Yeah, well we can SEE how you are." And on and on it went.

One particularly memorable morning for me, Uncle Eddie came downstairs and

I noticed he was not wearing his socks. His white ankles obvious above his brown wing-tips. "Uncle Eddie, where are your socks?"

He looked at me and grinned showing his side gold tooth. "Well, Jean, when I took them off last night I threw them up against the wall--and they stuck there. I knew it was time for a clean pair." Then he rolled his head back and gave one of those deep hearty laughs that I knew so well. Uncle Eddie knew he had hit bottom and he didn't like it. But by this time, he--or us--couldn't seem to turn it around. He refused help and we were doomed to watch him self destruct.

Some evenings he would go up to The Hammond Hotel in town to see all his friends. On one of these evenings--and none of us ever knew exactly why--he made a deal to sell the house, including all the contents. The family homestead that Grampa built and Uncle Eddie inherited. The house where my parents, two sisters and I lived--the only family Uncle Eddie had left in the house.

My mother and I were taking the Greyhound bus twice a week now to go to Lockport to buy him whiskey. There was no liquor store in Gasport. Uncle Eddie sat in what used to be Grampa's overstuffed maroon mohair chair with his bottle of Corbys next to him. He ate little or nothing for almost a year. He was only 47 years old.

One evening Uncle Eddie became violently ill and despite his protestations, my mother called young Dr. Cole. He came right away. And the news was not good. Uncle Eddie would have to be hospitalized. It was a week before Easter and he begged to be "home for Easter." Bargaining and buying time. Dr. Cole agreed. The next morning we found Uncle Eddie sitting in an overstuffed chair next to the space heater in the living room--dead. It wasn't long after that the entire family gathered round and Aunt Helen called a meeting of all of us children.

"Now, listen carefully. This is what happened to Uncle Eddie. His heart stopped. If anyone asks you how he died, you are to say, 'his heart stopped.'" We agreed. But Gasport is a small town and I'm quite sure that most everyone knew WHY Uncle Eddie's heart stopped. I think his heart had broken long before it stopped.

LEAVING GASPORT

It was the Ides of March when we left the family home in Gasport. My father had found an apartment in the City of Lockport on Church Street. Our rented truck held the few belongings that we had brought from Buffalo. With the exception of Aunt Helen's Baldwin Piano which did not belong to Uncle Eddie, the rest of the furniture in the house including the large oak dining room table and chairs, the marble topped sideboards, and the four poster beds had been sold to the new owner.

I sat in the front seat of the truck with Judy on my lap wondering how she would fare in the city. She was used to running in the fields and swimming in Mirror Lake. Now she would be a city resident along with us. My mother and sisters were in the new apartment getting it ready for our arrival. My father steered the big truck down East Avenue and I turned around to take one last look at the house.

Without my grandparents or uncles the house in Gasport no longer held the magic for me that it once represented. I had grown from a happy carefree child to one who, like my beloved grandmother, had suffered too many losses. Despite the sadness I still did not want to leave. I didn't want to let go of all the memories this house and this town held for me. I wanted to live in Gasport--or in the past--for ever. I wanted to lie again under the tall horse chestnut tree and remember the closeness of crawling on top of Uncle Eddie and hearing his deep laughter while his gold teeth gleamed through his smile.

I wanted to sit in the rocking chair on the front porch and comb Gramma's long silver hair. I longed to have Uncle Emmett pick me up and rub his whiskers across my cheek. When the snow falls I wanted to sit in front of the big black iron cookstove with my wet socks hanging on the side. I wanted to drink again the cool well water and taste the ripe juicy Richmond Cherries from the tree next to the well. I wanted to go down the road to the small bridge and sit there and watch the water in the creek flow under the hanging birch and willow trees.

I wanted to awake again on the feather mattress in the four-poster bed and hear the voices of my grandmother and uncles coming from the kitchen. I wanted to smell the bacon frying, the coffee brewing and the aroma of burning wood from the cookstove. Yet, I knew these times would never come back. Despite my hopes of someday buying this house my grandfather built and returning to Gasport, I knew in my heart that I could not relive the past.

The past was lived fully as a child lives it. Now I was 15 years old and part of me, the child part, was over. Only the memories remained. Memories that I have recalled in this book, but memories that are always with me--just below my adult facade.

DEGAN FAMILY TREE

Thomas Degan - 1866 - 1944--------------------- Mary Ann (Conners)1867 - 1946
Born Manchester (Preston) England   Born Gasport, New York

William, Thomas, Martin, Leslie, Edwin, Harold, Johnny, Emmett
Grace, Esther, Dorothy, Helen (Blanche Chaplin/cousin)

(William, Edwin, Harold, Johnny, Emmett - Never Married)

Thomas Degan   Martin Degan
(Elizabeth Templeton)   (Marian Zent)

William, Edwin   *William, Robert, Raymond, Richard*
                                          Virginia, Mary Jane, Delores

Leslie Degan
(Margaret
no children)

Grace Degan   Esther Degan
(Jacob Yerge)   (Peter Gormley)

William   *Thomas, Margaret & Mary (twins)*
                                          Nancy, Edwin

Dorothy Degan   Helen Degan
(Aloysius Kolb)   (Allan Casey)

Jean, Joanne, Mary Ann   *Susan*

Printed in the United States
by Baker & Taylor Publisher Services